SMART LIKE ME

SMART LIKE ME

High School-Age Writing
From the Sixties to Now

edited by

Dick Lourie and Mark Pawlak

with

Robert Hershon and Ron Schreiber

HANGING LOOSE PRESS

Published by Hanging Loose Press
231 Wyckoff Street
Brooklyn, New York 11217

Cover photographs by Joseph Szabo
Cover design by Alice Soloway

Hanging Loose Press is grateful for grants in support of this
publication from the Literature Programs of the National
Endowment for the Arts and the New York State Council on the
Arts.

LIBRARY OF CONGRESS
Library of Congress Cataloging-in-Publication Data

Smart Like Me: High School-Age Writers, 1966-88,
edited by Dick Lourie and Mark Pawlak.
       p.   cm.
   Poems originally published in Hanging Loose magazine,
issues 1-50, 1966-1988.
   ISBN 0-914610-59-7:   ISBN 0-914610-58-9 (pbk.)
   1. School verse, American 2. Youths' writings, American.
3. American poetry—20th century.   I. Lourie, Dick.   II.
Pawlak, (See above)
PS591.H54T94   1988
811'.54'0809283—dc19   88-1069
                        CIP

Produced at The Print Center., Inc., 225 Varick St.,
New York, NY 10014, a non-profit facility for literary
and arts-related publications. (212) 206-8465

PREFACE
by Richard Lewis

What this book reveals is a whole spectrum of fine poetry that could easily be submerged, or written off, as simply "adolescent" poetry. Too often the poems of high school students are printed, often by the students themselves, in school literary magazines, distributed to peers, teachers, and family—and then filed away and forgotten. Even our poetry "establishment" usually does not include or recognize the work of the young, referring to it as still formative, imitative, or without "poetic" merit.

It has been my experience that much poetry by the young, from children to those in their teens, is of exceptional value, not because it is, in some romantic way, by children, but because the young have a special relationship to language and poetic thought. They are often closer to the emotional and feeling elements of poetry—and, because of their age, use and respond to poetic insight as a means to sort out, explain, and define their relationship to some of our most primary human experiences. I am convinced that young people at whatever age, use language, if it has not been completely homogenized for them, as a "still-shaping" form of expression that can be, in the hands of the young, an authentic and honest means to say what they want and have to say. It is a language that has not been bridled, from the demands of our analytical education, with a false sophistication and tone.

Given the right kind of meaningful encouragement and support so necessary at any age, they can write poems which stand on their own as the real thing—and not a poeticizing of experience which sometimes becomes the trademark of older writers anxious to have their poems sound like the work of accepted poets.

The idea of this book is an excellent one. Besides the fact that it will bring to the attention of the public a group of serious younger poets, it indirectly acts as a model, and a source of real inspiration, for young people who (and their numbers are incalculable) are writing out of a genuine need to write. My suspicions are that many of these poems did not come from school assignments—but were composed from an individual urge to put down in writing what each of the writers was thinking and feeling at the time. They are poems that, as with any poetry that eventually moves us, were already gestating in the mind of the poet and had to be written.

In a time when the "adolescent" culture is too quickly condemned for complacency and illiteracy, these poems are saying something different; they range through the widest possible arcs of feeling and subject matters, and without an abundance of verbal virtuosity and pretentiousness, speak directly and simply with the conviction and energy of young people growing into their—and our—world.

INTRODUCTION

Hanging Loose, an independent literary magazine, was started in 1966. It has published continuously since then; the magazine's 20th anniversary issue *(Hang Together)* appeared in 1987. In 1975, Hanging Loose Press was established to publish books of poetry and fiction by writers whose work has appeared in the magazine. The press has published about 50 titles.

Since the first issue, *Hanging Loose* has been receptive to the work of high school age poets. Since 1968, every issue of the magazine has included a section of their work. This anthology is a selection of 148 poems by 50 of these poets, first published in *Hanging Loose* between 1966 and 1988.

When the magazine started, all its editors were active in, among other things, teaching poetry in the schools. Over the last 20 years, this involvement has continued. In our view as teachers working with poetry at the high school level, one striking and consistent circumstance has been the extent to which these young poets, as writers and as readers, are isolated from most of what is happening in contemporary poetry.

Of course their isolation mirrors that of the general reading public, to whom serious fiction, despite obstacles, makes its way more easily than poetry. And for those of high school age, the isolation has a further consequence, for a surprising number of them are in fact interested in poetry, although their access to it is so limited: in school they have probably read the English Romantics, Dickinson, and perhaps Whitman. If they have taken any "Honors" English courses, they may also have read T.S Eliot, or William Carlos Williams. But with the contemporary world of poetry, as it exists in the hundreds of literary magazines in this country alone, most high school students have had virtually no contact.

This means that when their interest in poetry is expressed in writing poems, they often write as if they were participating in a tradition that stopped developing 50 to 100 years ago. For many, therefore, poetry is something they "outgrow" partly because it has no living connection with their own experience, their own lives. Further, these young writers have correspondingly little access to the audience of other poets and poetry readers that provides for the rest of us—as is the case with any art—the support, comment, criticism, and community we need in order to maintain and develop ourselves as writers.

So when we opened the pages of our magazine to high school age writers, it was both to help reduce their sense of isolation, and to welcome them into the wider community of writers to which they have so little access. Most of them, in fact, don't even know that such a community exists. In addition, we wanted to share with our readers the surprising and sometimes extraordinary work that these young poets can produce (that, of course, is one of the purposes of this anthology, as well). It seemed natural, too, that when Hanging Loose Press began publishing books in 1975, two of its earliest titles were by authors (Katy Akin and Sam Kashner) whose work had been appearing in the magazine since their high school days.

Like all artists, the high school age writers in this anthology build their work in some substantial way on the base of their own experience. Their poems really mean something to them. This foundation of personal significance is one of the qualities we look for, as editors and as poets ourselves, in selecting any work for our magazine. With high school age writers, it is one of the qualities that clearly marks the poems we're interested in, distinguishing them from those that seem to have been written in response to classroom-generated encouragement, suggestion, or outright assignment.

The high school age writers whose work has appeared in *Hanging Loose* are already highly motivated; they seek *us* out. Their work is often highly personal, and always rooted in their experience, and in the need to write—nobody asked them to write; they do it anyway. One of the things that follows from this is the striking vitality of the poems. Another is their openness: these poets write because there is something they want to show us. What they want to show us, of course, may not always be what we want to see, again because what's driving the poems is not a theme or idea chosen for a hoped-for broad appeal to a classroom of sometimes reluctant students. Rather, it is (once more, as with any artist), something intensely important to one individual.

We believe this collection is unique. There have been anthologies of poetry for children, written by children and by adults. Richard Lewis' collections of children's work, *Miracles,* and *There are Two Worlds*, and Edward Field's translations of Eskimo songs, are some examples. And there have been anthologies of poems by adult poets chosen specifically for their appeal to high school students. Kenneth Koch's and Kate Farrell's *Sleeping on the Wing* is a recent and excellent example. But collections of work actually written by high school age poets are few, and none that we know of has presented the work of young writers in the United States collected over such a long period.

In a sense, all the writers in this anthology are contemporaries of today's high school readers. To us it seems that even the high school writers of 1966 can be called contemporary with those in high school today. Common parlance refers to "the 60s," "the 70s," and so forth, as separate eras. But putting this anthology together from back issues of *Hanging Loose*, we were struck by the realization that we could not tell by reading any given poem (except for the occasional topical reference) when it was written. The significant concerns, the freshness and vitality of language, seem consistent, from those writers who were adolescents in the late 60s to those who weren't born until the 70s.

This is not to say the poems here are uniform in their style, their tone, or their themes. Their diversity, in fact, made it hard for us to decide how to organize the anthology. In the end, we chose to follow the practice of anthologies of contemporary poetry: we presented each poet as poet, with all his or her work together, rather than scattered among different thematic or other categories. And we have presented them in the order they came to us, from Deborah Deichler in 1966 to Derek Miller and Rebecca Wolff in 1986. This is the simplest and least obtrusive kind of organization; it also enables us to give some order, through the brief biographies accompanying the work of each writer, to the extraordinary spectrum of what our high school writers have done and become since we first published their poems.

Although we hope this anthology will be of use to teachers, we don't see it as a textbook; one of its aims is to show young readers some of the work of their contemporaries that we believe can communicate directly to them and doesn't need the mediation that textbooks are designed to provide. Critical apparatus, questions, suggestions for activities could all, we think, undermine this aim by providing mediation and implying that it is necessary. Such interventions can become self-fulfilling prophecy.

Rather, we thought the poems could speak for themselves, both to the adult readers of this book and to those of high school age, as they spoke to the editors of *Hanging Loose* when we were first surprised and delighted to encounter them.

The Editors

CONTENTS

SECTION THREE: 1976-1979

SECTION FOUR: 1979-1982

SECTION FIVE: SINCE 1982

Section One: 1966-1972

Deborah Deichler

(UNTITLED)

When you are trapped in rabbit grass
   and it begins to grow up
      all about you
      with the speed of rain,
  never again
      will you find the way out
      you will be lost forever
  and the rabbits will smell
      you from far away
  and put their furry ears against
      your eyelids
         when they know you are
         asleep.

Deborah Deichler

(UNTITLED)

The King looked in the mirror
     and laughed
     at the old Skeleton
       he saw there.
     Go away,
       he said
And the Skeleton started laughing
     too.
     Come away,
       he said.
Then the King grew fearful.
     I cannot. Not yet,
           he said.
But the Skeleton stepped out of
     the mirror and
     heaved his sickle
       with all his might

into the King's forehead
And threw the pieces of the
        shattered King
                back into the mirror
                    and put on his crown
                        and started downstairs
                            for the throneroom.

Susan Mernit

PLEASE TELL ME WHERE THE CLEVER GOES

My self-confessing plaintive poems
        whose "I" repeats a hundred times
                are not directives like you write.
I remember very well,
        yet cannot think of the modifying times
                that threw you to some pages to
                        sit and write a poem.
        You write with a flashlight late at night.
                It's those rhymes that go on to die
                        as puns
    those jokes that should explode
        that always make me look up and ask:
        How do you keep them off the page?
    Just tell me so a million times.
To remember and decide:
        I once told you to be glad
            I said smile
        I said scratch
        I said drink milk
            I said decide
            I said clap hands
        I said nothing and thought that I was
                        silent, mythic as the sea,
            telling you I smiled and was glad.

But anyway I wanted nothing
    was happy, wrote poems,

20

did nothing,
and watched the small I grow.

Susan Mernit

THE PRISONER

1.

she is a girl who is trapped.
if her head could turn it would
turn to the left and back.
her eyes are open wide.
the fingers of her hand are
long, and gently rolling.
her pale folded nails
touch her palm and touch the air. the air
has the space of a kiss.
the kiss in the air
is the tip of her tongue.
the girl is ready to speak.
her red mouth begins adding
phrases to lips.
her mouth is the part that moves.
the rest of her face is a girl who is trapped.
her body doesn't matter.
she is a girl who might be small
or her legs might extend like
spider's sex.
if she is small she will look up and shout.
her size will say: "She is me.
I am the girl. I love you."
The red mouth will smile.

2.

I cry because I love you.
to say not body but mind.
the serpent inside
          the serpent's coils.

dank like afternoons and buses,
and twisted friendship in the flesh,
the hard-legged lover telling lies uptown.
the action is none.
she sits and waits and types some
poems. she drums his ragged voice:
what he is doing she doesn't know.
the small room where he flung his
tie and licked her heart is
still small. only she can see
the matted imprint of her
flesh, the stain on the bed.
that day when he bit her arms
he stopped to close the door.
their clothing on the carpet
was music floating out the window
to Broadway. their voices when
they stopped were love. the
river was not far.
she badly wants to touch those walls.
ripple her breast against the desk and
chair. the sink and mirror said you,
said red swollen lips,
were many kisses and smiles.
the smile she smiled was an
angel's. he said it was lovely and
small. the last touch of his arm
is still there.
she didn't know he would not call.
she went home and started waiting.
the days passed since she told her friends
she had a lover.
their smiles were her smiles in doubt.
her sin was he didn't call.
his sin could not have been love.
she loves him still.
they envy her this sadness.
though she eats well she frowns
and stops and smiles.
she would start to hear her lover's voice,
yet her sad mistrust would be love.
she is writing her story in a poem.
she wants to stop loving him.

it is the body inside the body that holds her.
it was the crime of his sleepy blue eyes
which made her wrong. it was his
drowsy passion which moved her.
his voice began to speak when they met.
on the subway to his room he didn't speak at all.
he rocked and shouted and folded his arms
and the train came and went uptown.
she didn't love him then.
she loved him when he spoke to her
when he turned his head and his face was fine
when she was afraid and pulled back from his eyes
the moment they first kissed
the timing of the pause as they kissed again.

she is always quiet in her house, in her pink
room. her eyes are larger, if anything,
and she laughs in crowds because her
face is too still.
she has been writing a story in a poem
and wondering what to do.
she asks only one thing:
what does he feel?
how can I make you see I love you?

Sam Kashner

•

When you come round
i wonder where i'll be
inventing the sunlight or
a telephone for the deaf
in a nursing home
with rooms always   available
the patrons leave
sometimes by coughing and
clawing at the air
or silently
without giving back the key.

Sam Kashner

•

combing your hair for you
is like Lewis & Clark
racing down the rapids
and coming to rest deciding
where to go, while this
tangled mass of country comes
alive inside my hands.

Sam Kashner

•

her eyes move   down the wall   like
fine   lines   of   light through
venetian blinds.   opening   the window
she lets the light drown her face
i'd swim out to save her but i'm half asleep.

Sam Kashner

•

your face is like a hospital
clean
smooth & starched
skin of alcohol and steel
with a place for weeping
for emergencies and tests
swiftly the mixture of joy and horror
can be seen during ''hours'' paying visits
to your face.

Sam Kashner

●

al capone had
over 900 white shirts
when he was sentenced to
prison he took them along
and in his cell once every day
he would drag the trunk from
under his bed and count them up.

Sam Kashner

●

we dance
against the
imagination
of the century
and we allow
religion to get
caught in our hair.
we are a weak
throated choir
and bring no one
to tears.
we watched the war
on television and
we remember the
buddhists shaved and
showered with gasoline
sitting on a corner of
the planet in saigon.
they would all leave their
bodies and stand on the corner
to watch themselves burn.

Sam Kashner

•

kissing you goodbye
for the last time
made me feel like
Sir Walter Raleigh
when he ran his finger
along the blade
of his own death axe.

Sam Kashner

•

my friends
all like to relax—
to sink into their
army cots and
sleep in a khaki colored
dream.
to spend korean weekends
on the sly
and to dream of their wives
as being almond-eyed
and gentle.

Sam Kashner

•

there was a time when
i would bend over backwards
for you
like an astronaut

riding his toy horse
between the planets.
but now i am just jealous
and jealousy is the sport
of old men
and those confined to
standing still.
i am jealous of your
clear face
and your history of
love affairs that you
number like a soldier
counting up spent shells.
there was a time when
i would bend over backwards
for you
but now with this jealousy
rotting in me like arthritis—
i can barely move.

i'm busted open
like a valley
with the cold light
of language traded
between us—
like two phoenicians
who experiment with
thievery   you remember
to hand down your laws
by word of mouth
not allowing for error
you just kiss the music
and sail away.

Sam Kashner

WHEN ARCHEOLOGY COMES TO YOUR LEG

when archeology
comes to your leg

i hope they find
the pictographs
i left there.
when winter came
i scratched a
calendar above the
white candy of your
feet.
and slept the whole
winter undisturbed
by falling rocks or
restless, refusing
bears

Katy Akin

THE EGRET

the barn-roof arches
an egret drops his webbed stilts
to grasp the beam—
white neck still questing air,

he stands; a norseman before me.

a pause—lift—
and up past pines
spreading his boomerang wings;

His legs are branches held behind
to meet the sea
cold somewhere over a hill.

Katy Akin

FINGERS

I
magic teeth
a dying camellia
shakes me
I am coming

II
chipped cup
reservoir
filled with my gaze.

III
I feel my mouth on fur.
dream of a green cat
pains me at the top of the stairs.

IV
you keep them wound like clocks,
the baskets, notes,
holders of gifts I have given you.

V
I am a ball bouncing in my own arms
looking for more rubber
red flesh

VI
a salt shaker
If I sprinkled it on my head
would my tongue come out
to look?

VII
I lift the cup to my mouth,
wanting to empty myself.

VIII
I would like to lie naked
in a hill of raisins.

Katy Akin

CAKE POEM

I feel good about cooking.
The planning, arranging
Of pots like waterbirds, pans like boats
Oars of spoons, lakes of boiling water,
Nobody watches me.
Flour collapses into milk,
A tree disintegrating into earth.
Egg yolks float
And there is the peculiar pleasure
Of breaking them, the yellow blood.
I pursue recipes
Like a child who must pick all the flowers.
Best of all is baking,
Putting the brown unformed mud
With all those beaten cells
The vanilla from South America,
The milk from how many cows,
The magic powder to make it rise,
Shutting it into warm gestation
The hot spirit-boat,
The directions have been observed.
Later it appears
Swollen, with a steaming crack.
I have given my fingerprints
To its invisible swirls,
My cake.
I have fashioned a planet.
And then the sharing.
Cutting a map
I give it out like countries—
And it feeds me.

Kathy Akin

WAKING

Three days I've lived in my new house.
I wake to find the grass already risen,
the agreements made softly plain.

the narrow finger of the street
points away from me now.
it is better
to spin around a palm tree
fruiting with crows.
grass stretches over the low windows,
the beetles walk through the door
from the field;
every morning plans to make me whole.

Katy Akin

VAN BROODJE'S COLORED WINDOW

hares with slashed bellies
hang below the sweet acid
of stained glass.
hares with fur
damp from terror-sweat,
hares with death-fur
growing over their eyes

below the beardsley curls
of languid leaded stain
hang hares
stripped to the marble flesh,
muscles humping the slick bone,
fur shoes still intact,
hanging in outsize clusters.

I like the pheasants too
dangling, feather antique dreams
bleeding into wooden shoes.

Katy Akin

CANJUANI—FEBRUARY

we look at each other
with rivers now,
the days
we walk down the road
into sure sun,
almond trees,
thick with white flowers,
feeding us
(we are an eagle
arms thick with feathers,
who dream of wings)

in our eyes
the master water,
on the road,
stones parting to show the sky.
the nights
we camp in the kitchen,
bread and onions
feeding us,
the ragged sleeves of the fire,
our solid voices
our flickering cheekbones.
the nights
we wear each other's bodies
like gifts,
and in the business of sleep
sweat, and turn over, and let the dreams fall in
like the night
through the little
high window.

That pale square
is all I see
when I surface alone
from the current of sleep—
it is letting the water in,
to fill the room;
the clear black water
is filling the room.

Rob Solomon

•

Have you ever seen a flock of geese fly by?
Or a nine inch amoeba
On a plexiglass sky light
In the roof of an octagonal cabin in the woods?

Rob Solomon

•

They have tombstones in their eyes.
Yes, you can tell they're doomed.
It is in the air of things;
even the alphabet soup says so.

Rob Solomon

UNFINISHED POEM

Vast purple trees.
Think of the starving.
I hear people are really starving.

No one say anythin'.
Shore they're cool.
They talk about acid and cutting classes,
Instead of talking about swimming pools.

"You know nothing."—E.G.

Everyone talks.
Talks about dope,
Talks about money,
Talks, talks, talks.
Why?

"Stay in school
Otherwise you won't be able to get a good job
When you grow up."
When you grow up,
Will there be a world to get a good job in?

"Ever since the industrial revolution,
The power of government has grown."   —Robert Jensen

•

Take yourself a seat on the world.
Put your feet up;
Make yourself comfortable.
After all,
It's your world.
You evolved,
Over millions of years,
To be a success in this world.
There's no reason why you shouldn't
Be comfortable,
The world is dying of hate.
Hate causes hate.
All we have to do is break the cycle.

If you hate the things you resent less,
They will resent you less,

And leave you alone.
You might get to like some of the things you resent.

The rabbit looks up,
Now smiling,
Pulls out his dagger and
Stabs himself.
He expires.
The foxes, mice, and
Finally maggots eat his flesh.
The bones are ground to calcium powder by the elements.
His hair remains for awhile,
Then is blown to the corners.
There is nothing.

Growing goes two ways,
Up,
And out.
When you stop growing out and only grow up,
You get rigid—
A "Grown-up."
Ceasing to grow out is the number one cause of senility
    in the U.S.

•

Reincarnated,
The rabbit rises again.
As a young child,
His home is moved to the big city.
The more he watches,
The better he sees through things.
The better he sees,
The less he sees.
Finally he sees so well,
He sees nothing at all.
At this point he becomes desperate and
Jumps off a tall building.
His body is thrown into the sewer.

Slowly gather yourself (the molecules)
Together.
Find the energy to open your eyes.
You see the light on the ceiling or
The stars.

Man,
As a tree,
Should spread his roots as he gets taller.

The play of *Macbeth* ended,
Only to start in real life.
It frightens me.

I saw an old face.
It glared for a while.
I feel guilty.

Feelin' fine ain't ya?
The trouble with floating in bubbles is:
When they rise too high,
They burst;
Leaving you to sink slowly through the ground.

Watching you:
Your face changes meaning as you grow.
I have grown to dislike some of your actions.

•

"He who laughs has not yet heard the terrible news."
—William Blake

Going through the routine of Mondays;
This one as every one.
Today seems strangely irrelevant.

I tossed the orange china pig,
Given to me by my arch-enemy's mother,

Into the air.
It fell and broke.

You are your reflection.
Choose your looking glass well.

Please!
Form two lines.
Step right up and get yer used brains.
Hate is also available,
At reduced rate.
Smile.
You are of the last generation,
I'm told.
You won't have children to suffer your sufferings.
Death will be their swift exit from the world.
Oh.
Please don't get lost in forecasts of doom.
There may be a safety,
Built into the universe's unseen pattern.
When there's nothing seen here,
Will the stars still shine?
As in the paradox of the fallen tree:
With the last atomic flash,
Will it be light seen
Or will it be energy?
The air begins to resonate with everything.
What will happen when we are all resonant?

Saturday night,
Sitting at home,
Alone.
I remember last night—

•

I remember last night—
A mad moment.
I eat an apple and reflect:
At Jeff's,
There were lots of people in the living room—
A banquet.
In the living room also,
A lamp of iron and colored glass,
Hung by a chain from the ceiling.
It cast good shadows.
People are spinning the lamp.
I spin the lamp.
Later, I say:
"If the walls moved instead of the shadows,
When the lamp moved,
People would be really careful of that lamp."

Once again,
In some other life,
Many levels away,
Is the rabbit.
He is in the woods,
In his place,
A rabbit hole.
There are two exits.
A fox stands by one;
The other leads to dread unknown.
Frightened by unknown,
The rabbit chooses the third of his alternatives,
And waits.
Trapped in the hole,
His wait must not be long.

"It furthers one to have somewhere to go."
                                    —I Ching

Section Two: 1972-1976

Michael Rezendes

AFTERNOON

An old man
And a small boy
Leaning against the rail
Of a bridge
Looking out over the water.
It is sunny but
Windy winter cold.
They have their coats on.

You must realize
That the old man
And the small boy
Are not close to you.
They are
Far
Far
Far
Away.
They are a dream.

You cannot touch them.

William Henry Hogeland III

A CELEBRATION

It was late, the house was quiet. Silently we
    watched the fire, our faces flushed from the
    heat.
Outside it was dark. Snow. Lone wolf howl wasteland
    night. Moors.
We sat on the rug in front of the stone fireplace
    feeding the fire with sticks. We said nothing.
The room was wood. A cradle in the corner, hewn of

oak for a woodsman's baby: Old, old. A spinning
wheel. And the thick fur rug. And the stone
hearth,
flickering on warm well-fed bodies in lasting
fire-bright.

William Henry Hogeland III

●

we run, hand in hand
across the illegal grass
in sunshine
we are almost naked

Naomi Miller

●

I'm afraid of going home
I'm afraid of losing friends
I'm afraid of being jealous
I'm afraid you'll know me someday
I'm afraid I'll cry if you hit me
I'm afraid you won't hit me
I'm afraid of growing old
I'm afraid my mother will die
I'm afraid I'll feel too deeply and get hurt
I'm afraid you won't know me someday
I'm afraid I'll lose my sex urge

I'm afraid you'll lose your sex urge
I'm afraid I'll get sick and die
I'm afraid there'll be more wars too many wars
I'm afraid the world will die

Time out
Out time
Time out

It's snowing outside
We could make love now
You're very beautiful
You make me happy
I smell honey
I smell tea
I smell you
I smell your sweet-waft sweat
I smell your dirty shirts
I smell the cat box
I smell the dirty dishes
I smell dust
I smell floor wax
I smell ammonia
I smell ammonia

Time out
Out time
Time out

I dreamed I got to know your lovers and liked them
I dreamed your mother liked me too
I dreamed we had an apartment together in a city I had
        never seen before
I dreamed I made love to Athena of war and wisdom
I dreamed I went to your house and you weren't there
I dreamed you kidnapped my favorite cat
I dreamed many times the world was ending and I
        couldn't find you
I dreamed you gave me a ring you knew was ugly
I dreamed you were cold to me and wouldn't come home

Time out
Out Time
Time out

43

Naomi Miller

•

A woman
offers me a blessing:
I'll dance at your wedding

When I get married
no one will cheer

The priest will say a quiet
ave maria
ignoring me

I won't beg him
to turn around
or to curse himself in wedding me
to the space I stand near

No one will beg me
not to slide beneath his robes
for comfort

I'll miss you

Naomi Miller

COFFEE

Find a girl now. Go and find someone drinking in a bar
   who measures you and take her home. Avoid the
   bedroom where you would think of me. Let her leave
   at dawn when she's finished—or let her stay until

sunlight, have her waiting to see if you make her
coffee. I know nothing of all that beyond what
I've learned from you; I know though that it's
not something you've been sucked into—you've drawn
it to yourself. When I leave you to your soggy nights
and three p.m. cadaver breakfasts—I won't try to
forget how you look or what you felt to love me.

Make her coffee. Or let her make you coffee; sip it,
blow on it, slowly drink it. It may or may not need
sugar. You'll judge her taste in sugar and pretend to
watch her over the cup's rim. She'll be perched near you;
your body feeling syphilitic, and you'll hope you can
make it to the toothbrush before she kisses you again.
She'll hand you in the coffee through the door; you'll try
sucking it up with your breath pulled in from the cup—it
will slosh onto the bed, maybe onto your leg.

You won't smile or be embarrassed. You'll pour the
coffee carefully over her back if she lies back
down again next to you. There will be no playfulness.
She won't scream—she'll frightened think of stories
she has heard, that were removed and from another
world: no matter where they stand in the eyes of
the world, everyone has someone they consider
perverted. She'll look at you surprised, her body
going a little tense with fear—and trying to hide
it behind a smile.

You too will smile, or else not. There will still be
coffee in your cup. Hot coffee. And in her cup too.
You'll wipe the coffee off her with the sheet.
And smile, deciding it was a joke. You'll
be aware, though, that your eyes are hard.
She'll try to ignore that, wish she had left
the night before—and yet feel relieved.
You'll get out of bed and offer to take her
out to breakfast.

Or when none of this happens you'll be scared
it will, and wish it would to demolish the
fear. ·

We won't think of each other.

45

Richard Carlin

WEAKNESS

Margy speaks to me sometimes—
I have to laugh
knowing I'll never hug her
or touch her thoughts
or even mingle with her breath
because I am so weak—
I am only a willow
and I have no thorns except
my eyes.
how will she accept me?
knowing my weakness
she'll have to laugh
while she pulls out my eyes—
I don't mind being blind,
it's losing my thorns—
my only thorns—
that makes me cry.
O Margy.   O Margy.

Richard Carlin

THE ROCK POEM

little rock,
soon we're dust.
the sparkle of the sun
is flying from us,
let us shine, little rock,
let us shine

if we feel the air,
let us fly
if we breathe the dirt
let the dust fill our dreams.
we will not live without pain,
we will not be denied.
how can you shine without tears?

little rock,
soon we're dust.
the soot in the wind
laughs with us.
we are caught in a city
filled to the brim
with stars and dreams.
let us sip from the night
the blood to fill us.
let us shine, little rock,
let us shine.

Richard Carlin

ROSCOE HOLCOMB, ONE HELL OF AN OLD MAN

old man,
your bony fingers are hard and tough,
this I know,
but your finger nails are stained yellow,
all those rotten cigarettes,
they've cut through the bark,
but they'll never get the sap.

ly crazy men give things up,
t to give things up,
I'm no old man,
can still ll cement molds,
and build your dams and your roads,
I still have hands,
even if the nails are old and rotted,
look at the muscles, not the shell.
I've had a pretty rough life,
bad men and bad women and bad liquor,
never beat me, no sir,
I've fought them and beat them
and hollered with 'em and sang with 'em,
and Lord, none beat me, no sir, none.
so look at my muscle, and tight skin,
and tight eyes, and forget my shaking,
and forget my yellow teeth,
and forget my bald head.
my grand-daughter, she's tough,
she knows the whole bible, by heart,
yes sir, by heart, everything.
she's only five but she knows the bible,
by heart, yes sir, by heart.
and she make her mamma work, Lord!
she fight, she kick, she raise a storm, Good Lord!
she's my grand-daughter, tougher than me,
although I can lick you all.

my breath is still good,
my hands, look at them, they can work,
they're good, good as any.
I'm no old man, you're the one that's old, not me,
I'm young, I ain't going to die, no sir,
not without one hell of a fight, no sir,
because I'm strong,
and even God is afraid of me.
they got the bark, but Lord they never get the sap,
no sir,
not from me, no sir.

Richard Carlin

FOR THE THIN ONE

you are so thin, it frightens me.
your cheeks draw tight
to your skull,
your eyes are small, hollow bones
searching for roots, darkness,
dry land.

throw your hands out
and catch hold of death.
his eyes are dried petals,
his lips have been kept
pressed in a book,
by some longing lover,
his heart is a giant,
echoing shell.

what beautiful stillness,
I am frightened by you.
there is some longing
so strong, so horribly perfect,
that it draws us into death
when our hearts are only
young and soft.

Richard Carlin

PORTRAIT OF DIANA AT 12 AND A HALF (WITH A GOAT)

you are a madonna
with your hair untied,
holding a baby goat
that strains to be released.

every motion of your hand
is a perfect fixed law.
every motion compensates
for the disorder of birth.

his face is full and blunt,
it is beautiful in the sunlight,
but yours is a dark fruit,
your lips are drawn tight.

holding the goat, you are shameless.
this is your love that is not a man,
stumbling on legs
that are young and weak.

Kate Lakoski

INSPIRATION

It comes like a burst of sun;
when the lights are turned on after a movie.
It comes like a gentle rain.
You had almost given up life, but the rain quenches your thirst.
It comes like spring.
The first robin wakes you up one morning, sitting on a tree
                                    thick with buds.

It fills my head with thoughts.
Confused and bewildered, I have to sort out the contents of my
cluttered mind.

It comes like dandelions.
You have just finished washing the floor, and a kid walks all
over it with muddy shoes.

It comes like a worm.
You hate spinach, but your mother makes you eat it because
it's good for you.

It comes like a present.
You expected the butler to do it, but you didn't know how.

Brian Butterick

•

my father tells me
about his days with the union
and how he could've been
president of the IUE
and I believe him.
he tells me that god
is an old
old man
who hurls thunderbolts at
unbelievers
and I believe
and his stories run like
cartoon characters
through my head.

my father tells me how he always wanted
to paint for a living
but never did. he says
he couldn't stand the
insecurity.

he plays the harmonica
and every note is sweet
and precise and careful,
no emotion
no mistake.

my father never kissed me—
he left that
along with the cleaning
to my mother.
he goes off
every day
and he works at sperry rand
testing radar and is very secure.

my father tells me that someone
has written ''Jews eat shit''
on the men's room wall where he works.
he is shocked.
I am not so easily shocked.
      he tells me what it's like to be a man.
      I am not so easily convinced.

Elizabeth Hershon

•

When I shaved the grass
it jumped back up at me.
When I fed the moon
it threw up on me.
I've been treated like a dead rock sitting
      under a house.
When I kissed the butterfly he shriveled
      up and died.
When I hugged the bear he rolled in such
      despair.
When I threw a rock, because of my grief,
      it jumped back to me and flew in
      my pocket.

•

raving madwomen
in white sheets
surrounding the midnight house
holding up their flags
and screaming
madwomen's gossip

one walks down
the white stairs
and screams her solo
waving her flag frantically
she carries a bible

onion-faced women
crying in the night
the women set fire
to their flags
throw them at the house
then run
shrieking like children

Elizabeth Hershon

THE BELLTOWER

the moon glistened through the trees
shining heavy in one spot
a bald spot in the middle of the field
showing a rabbit
the rabbit sat with his furry paws against his face
he rubbed his eyes and twitched his nose
crickets filled the field with one continuous sound

the rabbit sat listening
there was evil in his eyes
something lurking in his thoughts
he opened his mouth wide showing two rows of shiny sharp teeth
his mouth snapped shut
he puckered his lips as if preparing for something
then he ran
fast across the field
the moon chased his body like a spotlight
the muscles in the rabbit's body were tense
front legs moved first
then back legs followed
all in two strong motions
he turned down a dark country road
he turned and laughed at the moon who could not follow
        because of
so many trees
he licked his lips as he ran
trees made dark shadows much larger than the rabbit
the rabbit came to a town and ran through the streets
his feet made thumping noises that echoed through the town
windows were shut all along the street
animals and children were grabbed off the street and pulled
        into houses
one man old and tired sat looking out of a shop window
the rabbit passed
their eyes met
the man looked quickly away
the rabbit laughed again as he continued to run
he stopped in front of the bell tower
he looked up to the top
it was cold the air was frozen all around
a light sparkled at the top of the bell tower
he laughed hideously as he climbed inside a small window near
        the curb
he ran up the stairs his shadow was clear and dark on the stone
walls
the shadow grew as the rabbit climbed higher
the rabbit reached the top
where there was a small room
in the center of the room was a bell with a heavy rope hanging
down

the bell was round at the top and jagged at the bottom
the rabbit's teeth grabbed the end of the rope he jerked down
over and over
the sound rang through the town shaking the houses
the bell tower rang until the people of the town
descended from their houses with guns and ropes

Elizabeth Hershon

THE BOX

I

my father stands alone
his eyes are like mud
they slip past the moon
his face is rough like the sand
he makes a gesture
he whispers into the wind
he watches as the sea rolls over and over
he climbs another rock
his hand grasps a corner of the rock
he brings his whole heavy body upwards
he moves with the tide
he jerks his head to the sound of a gull
the gull lands in the sand it pecks on a shell
the noise is soft and constant
he moves jagged now
I go home to my house and paint my face
he goes home and cooks his shoe
he eats it slowly out on the porch
the bugs fly around the lights and
bang themselves against the windows

II

I watch the news at seven
Carters family has moved into the white house

a woman is raped and Allen Stanford has written a new cook
    book
the man accepts his world
he accepts his tears
his tears continue
the man worries a lot
he eats peanut butter and honey for lunch
he thinks he might need to diet
he jogs around the block
he lives in a box
a box my stepmother made for him to sleep in
he slept there one night accepting it
thinking it might be one of his wifes stages
its been twelve years now
he still sleeps wrapped in cardboard
outside the sun is coming up
he hasnt had any sleep
he thinks he might like to move to the mountains
maybe by an ocean
he knows if he goes he will go alone

Elizabeth Hershon

THE CROWS

It is silent here
now that the crows have been
beheaded and darkness is about
to embrace us
I watched it all
from a distance
as they wound their necks
in the ceremony
it was a long twist only
the priest survived it all

and now in my mind the
rain is falling and flowing towards
the creeks
how fast it moves
swift like your gaze
and I am reminded of better times
of your face in the bushes and the
spots of light that glowed and
stayed with me for centuries.
But the rain will wash it all
away, wash the silent screams
as easily as it chases the
trout downstream.

I'm here again
where you walked across the
street, it seems like yesterday.
And me wishing I was in Boston
we didn't notice the crows then
I screamed it's too late the
spots of light have grown around my face and in your hair and
made everything so unreal
I remember the fight and your fist slamming into the door
of your grandmother's house, then the trees grew around it
and enclosed it and everyone inside
and now they are lost in there because of your anger
and I am afraid of going mad again because I feel too much or
        so little
I can't tell which is which anymore
and now that the last mangled crow is being tied up and
the crowd is moving in I can hear the rain
splitting from the clouds it's pulling the darkness over us

Edith Hodgkinson

•

I locked myself in the closet
        and swallowed the key
    it has settled in the pit of my stomach
        and it won't move
            it is hard and cold
    people are calling from outside
                for me to come out
but what can I say.

Edith Hodgkinson

BABY SISTER:

        yesterday you ate the other half of my banana
  and today
        I looked into your diary
you've learned to use the words well
        but no one's shocked anymore
I'm glad you can get out your hate for me
    when I was your age
      I couldn't
  you frighten me you make me laugh
painted eyes painted lips fringed leather purse
  smothered in perfume
          how far are you going to go
    at night
        a tiny teenybopper
  wants momma to come and tuck her in
scared of the dark

        you can't be two at once
  because I wasn't able to be.

•

I would like to tell the neighbor lady
       that the newspaper boy
    threw her newspaper into her rosebush
and it crushed three of the little baby buds
           but I won't

I want to tell my mother that I love her
           but I can't
because at the same time I want to yell at her
           and tell her it's all her fault
I want my mother's attention
       and when I get it,
           I don't want it anymore—
       I can't explain
I want to befriend my sister
           but how can I   when she yells at me
                   and calls me names
                   and treats me bad
I want to be in perfect health
               but something in my body says no
   I want to run in the field of
       friends and laughter and freedom
but my shoelaces keep
               coming untied.

Edith Hodgkinson

•

       and you were the first born
               elder child
                   knowing all of tomorrow
       parents your earliest lovers
               shot you again and again
           with mirrors
       and now you bitch at me like an old woman

and you were the last born
the fighter Taurus the bull in your stars
they didn't think you'd make it
a tiny mark washing away to nothing over night
daddy drank mommy went dry
and now you bitch at me like a little girl

and I sit somewhere in the middle
tearing up my faces with my hands

Edith Hodgkinson

WHAT TO DO IF YOU'RE MAD
AT YOUR MOTHER

if you're mad at your mother
go out and buy an orange
make sure it is a Sun Kist orange
and
make sure it has a navel
where would your mother be without a navel that's how
she was attached when she was born
then
go into your mother's bedroom and find her lipstick
give your orange big red smiling lips
give your orange big brown eyelashes with mommy's mascara
then take a piece of tape and on your mommy's head
write the word, mommy, now your orange knows who it is
take mommy and make her all pretty
and give her bows and bells and pretty hair
(even if your mother puts curlers in her hair make her pretty
anyway)
then hold your mother very gently and very
softly   in your hands   make sure not to smudge
her pretty smile or break off her hair
then tiptoe out to your kitchen   say bye-bye mommy
and gently roll her down into the garbage grinder
flick the switch and listen to her scream, your momma,
listen to her burn—
she's gone now

Edith Hodgkinson

ABORTION SET

1.

    wonder if this   evil
        pain inside of me   could be a new life
     blood and baby's white skin
   small devil monster   I can
       hear it howling
         fear its hands at night
     clawing at my broken seeds
       smiling its toothless smile
  hiding in the curtains of my womb

2.

a new life,   a hatching
      the exploding of eggshells
        you'd come out newborn, a changeling
          and turn older
             into a monster
   eat me up and leave no blood
    I know I've been there

          don't want it don't want that
            flower to open and bloom
  and then leave me   in a sack
     of blood and milk and tears
   uterus opening and closing
     like a starfish after a jewel
tides of ocean sweep in and out
     looking for pearl seeds
and I'm dry   waiting
     should I should I
     let you hatch
     and rejoice in your juices

3.

I used to be your angel
        but now I'm just dirty
    wishing for wings
        or a dark, dark hole to hide in
sticky little girl scared of doctors
        and all them out there with dark knives
            help me,   free me
black birds fly against
                dark egg sky
                it mixes in me
    mirror of an old woman
            rocking in her broken chair
                could it be me
flies buzz in zigzag
        like strange blind men trying to knit
    footsteps shattering
            and I'm a bad girl
                a dirty angel
    stepping in this hot ocean world
    waiting, weeping into my
            musty borrowed skirts
    wanting someone to come and punish me

4.

if pregnant women cry
        do their babies melt out of them
    silent blue hands grasping the sides of my face
    and if
    pregnant women bleed
        do their babies float out of them
    in tight red elastic bubbles
        just pop and evaporate and be gone
    rainbow wishes

    it's so much stronger than me
        such an old learned teacher
    they'll call me a murderer
            and fill my brain with knife words
    and I'm scared
            cause I don't need no more sad eyes

5.

glass jellybean with hands and legs
    drowning into soda pop   dissolving into
        bubbles dissolving
    opening eggs to find new hatched red chickens
    walk into the room   why is life so hard
you question me and
    I don't know
        it just is today

6.

big gray hospital entrance   you hold my hand
    but I'm just a body
        alabaster bones   plastic insides
    foam rubber breasts   rosewood smile
laughing fat lady tells us not to ask
    about the major risks of anesthesia
    makes me sign my name   so they'll
        have an excuse when I'm dead
    lady in pink takes me down to surgery   she
    knows what I'm up to
    but I'm just a mannequin out for a walk   I'm not
    really here
gray door swallows us   you stand there
    so far away   saying good bye

    cold tile room
        mannequin sits in
        anxious spells has read the two
Time magazines long ago   waiting in stiff green smock
got dry heaves
    scared   no one knows
    like always
Two old women complain about not being able to wear
makeup

    they call someone's name must be mine
    laid out on a table   ready for their cutting
    two big blue kaleidoscope horror movie bug eyes
    staring down   short walrus doctor
sticks I.V. tubes in those pale arms

sucks out the whites of those
        mannequin eyes
    they're only marshmallows anyway
glucose bubbles and licks its way in
    whatever happened to coat hangers
    heartbeat echoes, drifting
awaken to a whole room of white naked prisoners
    barred in by cascades of oxygen and blood
how can a mannequin bleed like this
        soaking with sweet red wine
you meet me upstairs with violets
        we promised each other dry eyes but I feel like
    I've just stabbed you
you'll cry at noon when I'm sleeping
        and I'll pretend not to hear

7.

    you're back again   you honey cell
        moving into my ovaries
                without even asking
    you bite too hard   you're no good
        I've been thru this before   or is it
            just a bloody   deja vu
    hiding in the sheets   you feed me toast
  doctor shows me where the moon is and tells me
        how fertile I am
yes, lover   we're able to plant seeds
        but we're too careless
    we break too many flowers   dropping lives like
        pennies down the gutter
  yer momma says she knows and won't let me
        kill it again
will put her huge hands over my stomach
        and freeze it
    mistakes will make us prisoners   but no.
        your white clouds can't bind my wings yet

8. Apologies

    I bet you'd end up with blue eyes like his
        I bet you'd grow old and hate me

I bet your virgin skin would crack with my moaning I
        know I couldn't keep you warm and I'm
            not ready yet
        to share his blue eyes with anybody

9.

        it was just as hard the second
            time   maybe
        even worse to kill you
    small pink thing crying
        you were a small mass of words
                withering with red energy
            calling out my name
            I heard you in my dreams
        eating at me, eating to become
        redder   stealing my blood
    you, wicked how I   hated you
to make me crouch over like a small animal
        covered with broken veins
this time they threw me on
        white sheets flecked with my own
            blood from where they
                clumsy, shaking
        missed with their own needles
    left me bruised and cold
hung up Christmas ornaments
        on those white clinical ceilings
I tried to hide under my eyelids
            and forget
        wondering who they fed my baby to

Edith Hodgkinson

[SHE MUST HAVE BEEN CRAZY]

        she must have been crazy
            to let them do that to her
        baby in a green torn blanket
        they carried her in huddled in daddy's arms

she was scared of the shock treatment of being left alone
and they wore white just like her dreams
and their shoes made no sound as they
approached so you could never tell if one was
creeping up on you or not   and they say she
tried to hide in drawers   dancing for a spanish
girl who threw things and picked tangerines to
pieces in the closet   and they asked questions in
sweet voices   did you ever feel like killing yourself
we have a special room special room she spun
and she spun she said don't freeze my brain
popped pills they shot her up with rocket ship needles
lady tried to take her blood eight times and
she didn't feel it she didn't feel it   every morning
she washed her body in the shower and brushed
her teeth with shaking hands   colored dragons
dancing on the walls jewish mother in the cafeteria
said here pretty baby we'll see what we can do and
she soon had a pot belly like everyone else

sometimes they let her out for walks
and she'd stumble on country roads
trying to hear the trees but everything
was so far away so far away
she watched the others cut themselves
with cigarettes till the skin was red and raw
sometimes she could see the moon through her windows at night
she said over and over I want to go home I want to go home
and the yellow brick road's turned
to pebbled dirt
and the emerald city's all ruins
they gathered around her   why did
you do it   why how who
and they all wore white coats
just like her dreams,
just like her dreams

Section Three: 1976-1979

Susan Brockman

DINNER WITH THE FAMILY

Sitting around a table
is a dynasty of women
extending back through generations
It is Father's Day
but the lack of fathers
sits heavily

My grandfather
sullen and ineffectual
sits silent
while women talk
for and about him
It has always been that way
except after his stroke
when he talked and smiled
and the women laughed and coughed
uncomfortably excusing
his personable condition
as a sickness

My father
has been missing for years
having escaped
when I was ten

and my uncle's absence
is most strongly noticed
when a woman has to carve the turkey

My two.sisters
rush in
to perform the ritual
kissing of cheeks
something I have always hated
but I am hurt when one aunt

deprives me
of the honor
saying with a smile
"Oh no / not you
you always cringe anyway"

Mike Shulman

SUN COMES UP

The sun
  rises
and nibbles
    the wall
  licks its lips
    on the window
  plunges
    its teeth
      into
        shade

  and coughs up
    day

Mike Shulman

LAKE: SUMMER

I explored a
  lake   a town

  that was not a lake,
    not a town
  it was their faces
      crewcuts
    dirt roads
    old Chevys
  empty cylinders

ours were long
        paved
            new
    and full

they lived in a different
        year

there was a bridge
between us

    travelers would pass through
the town, down Route 30, across
the bridge, as if it were a vein

the lake was a pulse which we had all
        gathered round to take

        and the mountains
        waited patiently
            endlessly
                for climbers

    at night
        with chirping
        and stars
all would swallow us

        the lake the mountains
the town would swallow
            both of us

            them and we
            and the bridge

Gerry Pearlberg

TWO POEMS FROM THE MUSIC OF CLIFF SAFANE

(1)

You lie on your lousy bed.
The moon removes
itself from view behind
an awaiting
cloud.
The army blanket, wrinkled
and faded
falls off the bed
as you breathe deeply.
Discarded bottles
some still part full
(for once you were stoned
you stopped drinking)
lie about the room.
Dawn opens the sky
in yellows and oranges.
You dream of how it was
and wake to
the nightmare of how it is.

(2)

Tiny birds leaping from
branch to branch
until they collide
and form a grey
cloud.
It rains.

Gerry Pearlberg

CITY SHORTS

I search the darkness
of my pillow for a moon
made of white stone
that waits for me while I
sleep.

a moth falls from the sky
like a silent silver garbage can.
his eyes are only little
seeing-stones.

this morning
they cut down a tree
in front of my house.
a bizarre magic trick
that failed.
this evening I can hear it
moaning.

Gerry Pearlberg

IN A DREAM

in a dream i saw a sharp-toothed snail
gnawing on a leg of a highchair.
after it crashed to the ground
i watched the snail lick the
applesauce off its cracked shell.

Dream #1

we crunch on the night,
gnaw at the darkness that inhabits our own bodies
and scrape the meat off the skull of daylight.

#2

i slide on a collage of breadcrumbs
dropped by some eternally old woman
and fall into a smooth blue hand.

#3

a bottle of black ink
a blue bead
a candle
are on a desk
until a vacuum cleaner stalks them
they move like long blurs down
the long metal throat
until they are gone.

#4

do not speak
for the spider has built a web
on your teeth while you were asleep last night.
listen. the threads of nighttime crackle.

Gerry Pearlberg

BOXES

lined up,
stacked,
balanced. some
are hollow
the wind howls through them
others are filled and heavy
filled with candles or letters
or curtain rods
that strike the moon from sight. or only half full
with pennies that slip through imperceivable cracks

and roll like wheels across the floor
until they are impeded by another box,
one-eared rabbits in a box.
one-sided earmuffs in a box.
square shadows cast by a box. so sharp a shadow.
unrecognizable shadows cast by a clutch of boxes.
they can hardly contain their excitement
as they wait to be opened.

Heather Ryan

HERE'S TO YOU, AND HERE'S TO ME!

—for J.R.

and isn't it true you respect me
for knowing I wasn't wanted
and getting out, though rather belatedly?
(Dad had the good sense to evacuate
three years earlier).

and isn't it easier to love me
now that I kiss you goodbye
and hug you occasionally
and you no longer grab me on street corners
or pinch me above my knees
or feel you have to respond to me
the way you respond to Deirdre?

and isn't it wonderful
that I can see you as a person now
instead of the mother
I know I'll never have
(I've resigned myself to this:
you're not the mother
of my expectations
and I don't want to look for that mother
in anyone else).

I have your hand size.
Perhaps some day
I'll play the piano
half as well as you.

Heather Ryan

DOUBLE DATE—DRIVER UNIDENTIFIED

Friday night in the car
We all knew the song
Sang along, whispered, hummed
My phone number on a matchbook
Hidden with the roach clip and switchblade
Was under the seat
My blood sister sat in the back seat
Her red hair clashing with her maroon jacket
She sat with a guy
Who would murmur "fuckin' this, fuckin' that"
"Dig it," and "putz" at intervals

Heather Ryan

REACHING FOR THE SKY

In gym class we stuffed ourselves
Into blue suits with ballooning bloomers,
And were told to climb the ropes.

If we climbed and reached the top,
Touched the ceiling,
And climbed down the rope again
(Careful of getting rope burns
On our hands—no sliding),
We would be members of the "monkey club."

For Claire and me,
Touching the ceiling

Was no easier than reaching the sky
With that same hand.

She and I would climb
Halfway up the rope
And hold the position
For the experience
Of the rope rubbing between our legs.

We were no fools, Claire and I.
Those who clambered for a place
In the "monkey club"
Missed what we didn't.
And though we never reached for the sky,
We had a little piece of heaven
Halfway up the rope.

Heather Ryan

A MAN WALKS WITH A WOMAN

his fingers grasping
the back of her neck.
What sort is this?
No arm about the waist
nor intertwined fingers.
A strangulation from the back.
He presses when she
gets too witty,
reminds her she's *his*
and any pretty things
she might say are his
to show off to his friends.
An organ grinder and
his monkey. A magician
and his severed assistant.

Heather Ryan

ANGELICA'S BATH

Jelly plays with soapsuds
in her bath—makes
snowmen like Ken dolls
(no privates) because
she doesn't like making
breasts and complicated
networks of pubis. Jelly
doesn't know Sylvia memorized
all the ceilings over bathtubs
she bathed in. Jelly's
too excited about the water
and making man-tits like
her own undeveloped ones.
She writes her name
in the soapsuds, knowing
it will disappear.

Laura Kelsey

DAUGHTER TO MOTHER:
DULLED NOVEMBER

I have no time for oil paints
now. The grey cellar steps hide
laundry; the snow tires are
on my list.

Every day I drink coffee and
drive to where they keep you
in a little room
(healing, they say,
slowly).

I know what happened to
the colors for you now:
they were diluted by lists
of "things to do,"
"errands to run," "letters to write."

The oil paints are in the closet behind the silver polish.
Watercolors merge as I pass down the road—grey (dishes)
blue (laundry) green (hospital) dulled
(November).

Carole Bernstein

•

As hard as you tried
to prevent it,
I looked into your eyes:
And I thought,
They are blue.
Once I saw them caught
by a bright angle of sun
I thought,
They are green.
Then a day you had
mistakenly come close
to me closer than you
wanted to or
should have, I again
looked into your eyes.
They shone as blue-tinged ice.
But beneath—
faint   hidden
murmuring alive,—
a pale green rushing river
in your eyes, a pale green river
of dark weeds and mild fishes

swirling with currents that danced through the rushes
green and swirling with sun and life—
In your eyes I have seen the river beneath the ice,
And I am content.
For I know that it is winter now,
And I have only to wait
For the thaw;
For the spring.

Carole Bernstein

POEM FOR AUG

it's not fair
        I know we said (thought) we could handle it
but it's not fair
you and I live other people's vibrations and their clothes
        in their houses with their daughters and unanswered let-
ters
and give warm mouths to each other as other people every Friday
        spot an eight for the benefit of the ticket-buying public
        (but never know we feel it in our vitals) (let them
        never know)
it's not fair (later playing me I walk down the empty
        streets to my own room on Avenue L
and dream of your dark warm bed on Avenue K)

Carole Bernstein

MESSAGE

you bastard
I have a terrible
how could you ever
aching for you that
treat me this way I
never is soothed and

hope you drop dead you
when I draw near to
aren't worth dirt and I
you I feel as if
never want to hear
big beautiful balloons are
your cursed name or
trying to fly out of
see your ugly face
my soul in unbearable joy
again
but I know you won't understand this

Lawrence Stazer

AWAITING THE AUDITOR

the security and exchange commission
splits open like an oyster
there are no pearls

the day holds still and the
stream of life runs white

bums steam open like rotting wallets

Lawrence Stazer

SUN UP

the sun's up to the fourth slat in the blinds
the cat stretches and lies on my lover's legs
the clock ticks slowly toward six o'clock

when i was a boy, grandpa
your shiny grey beard, your wise blue eyes
and the way your nostrils flared at dinner
when my little league team had lost
you were a lighthouse when the dark days came
now your mangled body, the foundations of my heart

Lawrence Stazer

A DAY IN THE COUNTRY

O dogshit, nothing like a sweet red rose
O shit, how unreflective and unlike
the cool still pond

Why don't sidewalks flow like green hills?
Why don't cars move silent as cows?
Why don't buildings burst into leaf?
Up the plow, down the jackhammer

To be buried alive!
To feel the root of the
blueberry bush
tickle my nose

Lawrence Stazer

HOMAGE TO THOMAS HARDY

And I saw dunes as high as mountains
The lovely lovely lovely little lilies

And boxes of windows, pockets filled
with doors. Everything knocking knocking knocking

The oval out of plumb, the biting cold
biting her cheeks   the birds

flew like dying dogs
My hands are wings

My foot neatly in my back pocket
I rode in the wind

My head bounced softly

Lawrence Stazer

CISCO

he was tired that morning
a sleepy texas town
with tumbleweed in the streets
and barmaids with lace garters
didn't tempt him at all
only vodka and milk
to bring out the stars a little
in his clouded head
and last night was there a last night?
Caramba

Lawrence Stazer

MONDAY NIGHTS

I hate Louise, I hate red hair, what's left?
Fat bears eating jelly donuts

The roof shingles are falling
And just whom are they falling on?

Lawrence Stazer

ALGERIA, 1972

i hear nothing, for my ears are blocked
i see all for my eyes are open
i speak not for my mouth is stuck
i shit not for my bowels are blocked
i wander in the everlasting night
a stranger to this town
and stop just stop
and be absolutely still
and gather dues until I might be
a chair a boulder a toothbrush

Lawrence Stazer

LIKE A CHOCOLATE

Like a chocolate bar melting
in the pocket of a heedless child
your love is wasted on me
a cold stone round and flat
warm room damp fire

Like a hard candy that will not melt
even after days of the tongue
tongue melts candy melts
warm tongue cold room

Lawrence Stazer

EPIPHANY

Puddles of rainbows on the roof

Santa Claus drowning in red white and pink
The stink of dead reindeer

And all through the house
Rats! Nobody watched for the rats
and the crow, the crow, the spider-colored crow

bites and pecks
bites and pecks
a detente in Hades
bites and pecks

Tammy Boyer

SPRING CLEANING

My mother neatly folded
all my old clothes and placed them
in four crinkly old paper sacks
clean pressed and perfect
just like they did with Nana
when she died and they laid her
in a soft pink coffin, all
satiny and slippery—

—It's not that the clothes are
no good anymore—I'm sure
some little girl would be happy to wear
a perfectly pressed pastel dress
like the one I wore to church
one sunny Easter morning

—It's just that my mother says
we can't let all those old clothes
clutter up the closet—we need to
send them away to make more
room for new clothes

I guess she's right
—I guess you can't let things
sit around and start to get
all cluttered up—so down the stairs
goes Mom with those crinkly old sacks
filled with the last mementos I have
of country hikes and penny bubble gum
and lonely recesses sitting on
an old rusty swing—

—and I can see a man down there
throwing all my mementos into
that huge Salvation Army van just like
the garbagemen toss out trash
into their big machine every Friday

and I figure they might as well
take it all away—my closet
was really kind of getting crowded
anyway, and I might as well let
bygones be bygones

Tammy Boyer

●

I am facing the dawning sun in the west while
the nuns trudge in solemn procession
thru a candlelit hall of a medieval church
as my eyes are fixed on a doric column
and the day has broken—the airline terminal
bustles with human beings really going
nowhere, except for Willard, who tells me
everything is going to be all right—
But I run to my mansion anyway, with my
dog (or is it a cat?) and stand on the
cliff, looking over a restless, stormy sea
of froth and brine wrestling in sinuous
knots, charging toward me and my cat (or is
it a dog?) and entrapping us in its
tangled web of confusion, and "nothing is
real, nothing is real, nothing is real. . . ."

Tammy Boyer

THE SUN WORSHIPPER

I've just come from the pool with
my bright orange beach towel, wet
with tiny beads of water like
a fresh dewy melon encased in
a cornucopia of morning sunlight
from which i imbibe the sweet

juices into the hills and vales of
my body—my knees, my hips, my
breasts—insurmountable everests to
the ants—the ladybugs, the men—
who stare in awe, just wanting to
climb, to feel, to experience the
thrill of reaching the peaks to
rise above the earth into a violet
mist of an unimaginable elysium,
from which they never want to
come down but must—slowly, gently,
to ease the pain as they drift out
of my mind as I awaken to the dreadful
pain of a sunburn

Kathy Buyck

•

My father and I are prisoners.
This school is the prison.
I walk in the front foyer and notice
    the doors are never locked.
My father and I escape and get picked up
    at the corner by Lynn in her blue V.W.
Lynn turns the corner and runs into the pole.
We are caught.
Again we escape and are on Glennmary Drive
    in our white Renault. (It is spring.)
We go up a hill then get out and walk.
We hear the people from the prison chasing us
    so we start up the hill through the weeds.
I notice a pool and because it is snowy and cold
    I suggest we get in it to keep warm.
The people from the prison are coming closer.

Kathy Buyck

A SILLY DREAM

I am a stuffed teddy rabbit.
Mom is a larger version of me.
Beth Fisher is a stuffed teddy bear.
Her mother likewise.
We are at the bottom of the ocean.
We live on a mesa and it has a ramp like
    a piece of land attached.
    This is our home.
Beth and I are playing ball, a seahorse
    swims by and we greet it.
Beth hits the ball and it goes into quicksand.
We go near the quicksand but we can't
    retrieve the ball.
I walk out on the quicksand and it is solid ground.
I retrieve the ball.

Kathy Buyck

A WEIRD DREAM

I am halfway down the hill and I want to get to the bottom
    fast.
I start to run, it's as if I'm trying to run against a force.
That force pushes me down and I end up crawling.
I get up and start to walk again.
I start to run and end up crawling.
I finally get to the bottom after crawling about six times
    because I tried to run.
I go into the party that's in the trailer at the bottom of the
    hill and they need something.
I end up getting it.
I have to go up the hill to get it.
I run and end up crawling.
I get up and walk, try to run again and crawl.
I am continually trying to run and end up crawling.
I'm halfway up the hill.

Section Four: 1979-1982

Allison R. Polly

●

Before she asked to go
she could almost taste the smell of elephants
She entered the smog filled stadium
shocked to really be there
People blocking her view
Men shouting "Popcorn, soda"
The yellow clown on stilts
stared her in the eye
It was the circus
The smell of manure
85¢ hotdogs
The thrill of the woman
with the half exposed behind
slithering up the pole
The crowd cheering as the acrobat
misses his catch

Was it the stunning Bengal tigers
that dragged her there?
Or was it him—
the gorgeous one
with the chain

Sarah Waddell

●

that bum is late
when I got all dressed up
in expensive clothes

he says he's fixing
his damned stupid car
when he finally gets here
he'll be so stoned

he won't be any good
to anyone

I should put on my
potato sack
mess my hair up
and wash off the Calandre

Sarah Waddell

WORKING

I folded bras
all day yesterday
while it rained

red, fiber-filled bras
for ladies with
huge tits

the ceiling leaked
and the bras will
smell bad tomorrow

I'll throw them away
in garbage pails marked
40 DD 38D 36C 32AA

but it is better than
watching
poor black women shoplift

Bonnie Campbell

•

In the study hall, amid the roar
of fifty paper airplanes, copper
hitting the tiles, pens scratching
through lacquer, one little fly
calmly walks across Russell Kelso's
back. It appears to be wandering
among those geometric shapes with
no purpose at all. However, I've
heard that a fly will drop eggs
when it lands. I wonder if Russell
will have a million baby flies
sitting on the squares by the
end of the day.

Bonnie Campbell

•

If I peeled you, my dear,
    grabbed the skin under your left ear and pulled,
I think I would find nothing but pulp inside.
    Like a radish
                you're bright on the outside,
                bitter on the inside.
Or maybe you're an onion, a long-stemmed onion.
                Onions make me cry.
I'll replant you in the ground, bulb down.
Maybe a goat will come and eat you.
                If not, I'll watch you decay.

Mark Duckworth

BUBBLE GUM ADDICTION CLINIC

Dozens of people
Scattered around the room
All craving the flexible material
Scarred lips
Mark the mature bubble-blowers
The door opens
A man staggers in
A popped bubble smothers his face
He falls to the floor
A new patient

Mark Duckworth

TEACHING AFTER HOURS

The bell rings
The students file out quickly
Except one
She slowly walks
Past the teacher
He winks
She winks
It's set
Teaching
After hours

Mark Duckworth

SUMMER AND CINNAMON

i cough
and spit up
favorable seasons:
summer and cinnamon
when times
tasted better
than i think
they ever could
again

Joanne Avallon

•

Five garbed nuns, black silhouettes
except for the shiny white headbands
that keep their veils in place
climb up the hill of my hand
in the moonlight shining through
my window.
On a pilgrimage to the glass of
water sitting on the sill,
they glide along, the short, fat one
leading.
When they reach their destination,
they fall and cling in religious fervor,
while I drink. Then, glass emptied
and replaced, the sisters journey back
to the white convent made by my
sheets and file
gently in.

Joanne Avallon

DAUGHTER

There is nothing to be said
for a daughter who comes
home at night with poems
on her breath.
I've noticed the ink stains
on her cigarette fingers and
her attempts to hide drunken
metaphors with simple words
and plain talk.
But I know she's spending her
time in a den of words,
on cushions of imagery,
making sweet love to the common
with her perfumed phrases.

Joan Polikoff

LATE SEPTEMBER, 1976

late summer beats its rhythm out with the crickets
                    and flowers fade
        the blue days are tinged with something else, now
            the lick of autumn rising,
and the children on the streets have worn jeans
                    for the past few days.
    a cat curls on a stoop, tail twitching,
                and sniffs the changing air.

        there is a cricket
        caught in my house.
                I can't find him.

Joan Polikoff

WYOMING

Space falls away on either side of the road
like wings of a bird
                 dipping
my eyes lull to the familiar monotony
of green sage
and far-flung plains.

                 the sky is a loose sheet
tied to the hills:
                 the care a lonesome animal nosing
through the meager dust-blown towns
                 that are gone when you look back
                            (if you do)

Beulah, Wyoming; population 40.

Joan Polikoff

ONCE, VERY LATE

the night is quiet
   and the light falls on the planes of your face
leaving the outlines in shadow
   you are only across the room from me
yet the distance wavers,
      and I know that if I walked to you
      it would be a long journey.

Joan Polikoff

STILLNESS

To be as part of a painting
        simple lines where sand
                meets water
                meets sky,
        dip of a gull.

  the whole world is still at that moment,
                suspended
    afraid to break the glass.

      but you bend then, unknowing
  to pick up a shell, a stone
      and the gull breaks its simple stillness
  arcing into the pale misted sun
      the waves curl again to the shore,
            grey sky shifts.

Jed Hershon

SATURDAY AT THE CATSKILLS, 1975

1

9:05: wake up, go to the bathroom.
9:10: wake up, go to the bathroom.
9:15: wake up, go to the bathroom: stay up.
You're the first one up, and it is *very* dark. You turn all the
lights on, but it is still dark. You can't sleep, because you're
excited about the day ahead. You lie on the couch, *very* tired.
You hear noises outside. The badminton net is hanging half off.

2

10:00: Ron & Dick are up, making coffee, and talking business.
But it's all double talk to me. Emmett's been up for half an
hour and is at John's. Dick drinks all the coffee. Bob walks in

the door, looks in the coffee pot (after going to the bathroom), and says, "Where the fuck's all the god-damn coffee!" He is kidding. But in a way is serious.

3

11:15: Carol is not up yet, and Emmett's out in the garage, getting the card table. Everybody else is talking about the magazine. "All right," says Bob, "let's take a short break, and then we'll start work." More coffee is made.

11:45: "Dad, let's play badminton.'
"Not now, Jed, I'm drinking my coffee."
11:50: "Daddy, let's play badminton!"
"Not now, Jed, I'm drinking my scotch."
11:55: "Daddy! Let's *please* play badminton!!!"
"Not now, Jed. I'm drinking my wine."
12:00: I give up.
"Jed, let's play badminton."
"Not now, Dad, I'm drinking my coke."

4

12:30: Carol *still* not up yet.
"Let's start brunch now," says Dad.
"We're gonna have a little brunch now."
"All right, let's have brunch!"
12:45: We start breakfast. Emmett is cooking, Ron is cooking, & Dick is making coffee. Bob is making toast.
1:05: Carol *finally* wakes up. Emmett has woken her up. They call each other cute, little, nice names. "Goo-goo bird!" "See you later Goo-goo bird! Ha ha!" he whispers.

5

2:00: "Maybe I'll go see George!"
"That's nice, Jed," says Dick.
"Maybe I'll go to the 'Fun Tunnel.'"
"That's nice, Jed," says Ron.
"Maybe I'll go swimming!"
"OK, Jed!!!" shouts Bob.
I'm bored. I'm bored. I'm bored. I'm bored! "Stop eating, Jed!" yells Bob. "You've eaten almost 6 sandwiches." Carol has gone shopping.

4:30: "I'm gonna make a phone call. I'll be *right* back."
4:50: Dick comes back, and they start again. They work long hours.
"I'm going to the Old House," says Jed.
"OK," says Dad.
"Goodbye," says Ron
"Goodbye," says Dick.
"Goodbye," says Emmett.
"Goodbye," says Bob.
"Goodbye," says Jed.
I go two steps away from the house, and I come back, for no apparent reason.
"That was a fast trip," snickers Bob.
5:30: Dick starts to say something. Bob interrupts. "Can I just say something here for a second? Thanks."
"Wait, Bob, you interrupted me, and I don't like that."
Dick continues, pointing out Bob's mistake.
6:00: Dick still talking. "*That's* why I don't like that."
"I'm sorry Dick, I'll *never* do it again," Bob says sarcastically.

7

9:00: They finish working
"Let's eat dinner, OK?" says Bob.
"OK," says everyone else. Except me. But I don't *really* care. We finish dinner. But I don't eat much, because it has curry in it. I eat cookies instead.
9:30: "Let's all sing!" says Bob.
"OK," says everyone else. Except me. But I *love* to sing. I like to sing. My father sings louder than anyone else. But I don't care. He likes to sing. He loves to sing. He loves to sing.
10:00: We are still singing. Everybody is happy. Everybody is singing. Suddenly, there is a draft that blows through the room. "Let's talk about the magazine," Bob says blankly.
"OK," says everyone else. They are like robots. I am left all alone. They talk for an hour.
11:15: They are still talking. I am dead tired, but it is my obligation *not* to go to sleep. To bed. Another draft, and my father jumps up & says, "Hey! Let's all sing!!!"

"OK," says everyone else. They start singing again.
12:00: Midnight: wondering why I am like I am. Never had glasses, braces, or broken bones.

"Jed, you better be getting to bed soon, go brush your teeth."

"No!!" I shout. "I mean, no. Hey, let's play darts!"

"No, Jed; you have to go to bed now."

8

1:00: Everyone is playing poker, and laughing. I am in the guest house, reading "Buck Rogers."

9

2:30: Everyone is in bed, except Bob & Carol. They are doing a crossword puzzle together. Then they play scrabble. Then darts. He doesn't play darts with me. They always make jokes, about going to bed together. I wonder. I pretend to go to sleep.

4:00: "Boy, I'm beat!" says Dad, walking into the guest house. I quickly pretend to go to sleep.

4:30: Wake up, go to the bathroom.

4:40: Wake up, go to the bathroom.

4:50: Wake up, go to the bathroom.

5:00: Wake up. Stay up. It's dawn. Stay up.

Tim Robbins

JAZZ 42 BOUNDLESS

(for John S.)

I'm hunched over the sink
like a hobo hunched over a cup of coffee
bare chested
I'm hunched over this sink.
The coffee is hard and black,
hot, he blows thru his blue lips.

The wisps of steam circle his face.
The wisps of steam are trailing
behind a desperate locomotive.

I gaze fathoming
the future in a sink of dirty water.
What a handsome lad I'll be   What a
lot of dirty water   Scissors
and whiskers.
I can see the tangled wet locks
shadowy over closed eyes.
A fly buzzing over crossed meditative hands.

The hobo is coming out of the diner.

He will wait until clouds cover the moon.

Tim Robbins

COUNTRY SCENE

After nirvana,
        any dreams?
After parinirvana
        memory *of* dreams?
The faithful horse carries us within
sight of the inn.

She dies along the roadside while we
roast and snore in public beds.

She who is more holy
        than our holiest bones.

Tim Robbins

THE BOWER

This spring we missed the lord sauntering
down Broadway whistling the Ode to Joy. We missed
his funny black umbrella and the way he played with
his watch chain when he stopped to say hello. We
missed seeing him in the soda shop bent over his
chocolate sundae, cursing flies.

But when the summer came and the bluebirds
played outside the window, and the squirrels
bashfully ate nuts from our hands, and the
neighbors' old she-dog gave birth to 12 pups;
we smiled and forgot about him.

Tim Robbins

THE PUNISHER, IT IS HE THAT IS ASLEEP

God incognito   dark sun glasses
a new name   new i.d.
fake driver's license.
He smiles walking down the street and in the drug store
and in the supermarket
                          down the aisles past the meat counter
walks in daylight
and no one points at him passing
or follows him hounding
for an autograph.

God smiles knowing the punisher asleep
with the sleep of death
and himself alive with the thought of life.

Duality,
He's been through it and condemns it.

Tim Robbins

WHY PEOPLE PULL THE BLINDS

People pull the blinds
to signal the end of day—as though
they were lowering the sun.
They like to lay down the sun,
tucking blankets up under his chin
and whispering him sad lullabies.
People pull the blinds
to signify that they are closing shop,
and if you want to buy
or if you want to sell
you'll have to come back tomorrow
after 9:00 but before 5:00
because at 5:00 the blinds will be pulled again.
People pull the blinds
to prevent curious neighbors and unblinking
alley cats
from watching them undress and lie down
and masturbate and re-dress and snore.
People pull the blinds
to keep out evil spirits of insurrection,
and people pull the blinds
so the right hand won't see
who the left hand is with.
When people are in a good humor
they pull the blinds
as though they were pulling a friend's leg,
and when people are in an ill humor
they pull the blinds
as though they were pulling their own weight,
and when people are angry with their god
they pull the blinds
as though they were pulling down the walls of Jericho.
People pull the blinds
because there are no more frontiers,
and it is better to face the void
a little bit at a time.
People pull the blinds

as though they were pulling leaves from fig trees
because in the presence of the moon
they are ashamed of their knowledge.
In the inner city
people pull the blinds
in mysterious Morse Code patterns:
SOS SOS THE TOILETS ARE OVERFLOWING
COME QUICKLY!
In Egypt people pull the blinds
so the lord will know to pass over their house
when he goes on his midnight raid.
He's busting all the first-born.
When people are in need of censure
they pull the blinds
as though they were pulling teeth.
When people have been through too much
they pull the blinds
as though they were pulling taffy.
When people are in control of their destinies
they pull the blinds
as though they were pulling the strings.
That is how and why people pull the blinds.
People pull the blinds
so that they can raise them in the morning.

Tim Robbins

I IMAGINE FUTURE LOVES

Oh
summer I
call you Michael
of the imagined
a boy I was
who played a ukelele
and pondered
all night away
with Joey interpreting
Beatle lyrics
reading between the
lines of life

fragile life line.

Michael is in my brain
and I know him.
He is an actor.
But Joey
Joey who left me for America
and nothing,
Joey where are you
and do you
still have the cowlick?

Tim Robbins

STAND WITH LEGS NAKED

Stand with legs naked in beatific sneakers
newly awakened look out the window
on the sun frosted streets of America.
All day long you dream of the monstrous angel
the well meaning beast.
All day long you hear a soft urgent voice
"Hold on, earth, hold on by your teeth.
Keep your mouth closed.
Who gives a damn why Bodhi-Dharma came to China?"
Sneakers will rub the celestial pavement.
When the idea of real estate passes away
to heaven, to hell, to a land of new opportunity,
trees will continue their patient ministry
to nagging birds.

Tim Robbins

from THE HOT TUB

A brunette wearing a lettered T-shirt, denims and thongs.
A boy. "Come to Magic Island! Come to Coney Island!" Big
red letters. He was leaning against the high wooden fence nibbl-

ing timidly on a green apple. His slight brown curls against the red wood board outlining a pale mid-western face.

A night warm with spring and sparkling with stars. Night too sharp, too distinct for a painting. Yet too formal and too perfect for nature. Very round. The scent of invisible lilac blossoms starting out into the air. The purple perfume brought to his mind images of sunset whiteness nakedness.

Much too round.

Whiteness and nakedness. A band of adventurers at the ocean. Young boys without bashfulness lie drying in the sand. Two-toned sand.

He scanned the vast black sky. The constellations— Orion, Ursa Major, Ursa Minor. He couldn't recognize any of them. Pearls and pearly pinheads glimpsed between rattling foliage. Indiscernible to him.

Timid. The apple had a flat taste. Not an apple yielding an abundance of golden juice to the harmless human tongue. He had once been used to apples of that sort. His great grandmother had had a wily old apple tree in her back yard. But his great grandmother had been dead now these four years. Deum Deum rest her soul.

He (the brown-headed boy) began to sing. He sang a song which he had known for as long as he could recall. A childhood song—yet a song which no child ever fully understood until he was no longer a child.

One is sitting, calmly reading in a room in a house. The room is of a subdued but warm yellow which radiates from some far away source. Some place where there is laughing. Cheap reproductions of Constable framed in plastic adorn the walls. The light of an electric lamp reveals the textured pattern of the paper on which they are printed. Sitting on a sofa beneath this lamp, one is unable to realize the complete nature of one's environment

unless

until he puts aside the book, rises and leaves the room. Until he opens the door and steps outside.

The boy now in the doorway with a frightened eager hand trembling on the knob. With time we go for the source. We come to require laughter. "Peter Pan, Peter Pan, sleep in Never-Never Land."

His singing was an ugly noise. He was at the uncomfortable age when a boy's voice, seeking to find a new form, temporarily loses itself. A description which is applicable to more than the voice.

Roundness.

Seven naked boys on a grey beach. Their bodies spindly and white. Unscarred by age. How do we achieve security in old forms—freedom from the development of new forms? Seven naked, breathless boys. The cool, grainy sunset. And the body is giving us signals. "Go forth from this placid sanctuary. Go to the cities. No more summer by the shifting oceans. Go to Magic Island! Coney Island!"

"What are you reaching for? There is no one behind you."

"These are matters of the divine, boy, the divine."

"Come to Coney Island," say red throats.

"Peter Pan, Peter Pan,
You got a peter.
You must be a man."

The boy closed his eyes and muttered the final line of the song under his breath. Then he tossed the half-eaten apple over the fence and turned his gaze starward again. He thought he had a good idea of which was the big dipper.

Tim Robbins

RHYTHM AND AFFECTION

A perfunctory dawn
lights a detached finger
drawing circles in the dust
on the night stand
beside the bottles.
Two men gamble rhythm and affection on one word.
It is silent now—not a car   not a clock
and in my memory the silence
of the song we heard last night.
Nothing can be said in my defense.
I've always been a sucker for a good love song
or a bad love song
eternally setting myself up
for the heartbreak of a half-assed dawn
groping for the chorus of a mediocre song

a radio dial hovering between two frequencies
eternally eternally tripping the verse
losing rhythm and affection
on one false move.
Back from the bathroom and he sleeps still.
The perfunctory dawn has entered his open mouth.
On his tongue I read not his dreams
but my disappointment.

Tim Robbins

YOU KNOW AS THE STREET KNOWS

The rain fills in the holes left by our serious walk.
The night turns casually and pauses
for a lunar signal.
I stand on a muted curb, dumbfounded.
I watch your leg disappear into a grey taxi.
How shall I imagine your face in a tavern somewhere
determined and numb?
How shall I reconcile your former exuberance
to the slow hangdog air of lacquered rooms?

In my own damp room I muse before the window,
remembering how you waited beneath the hotel awning
with neon-swathed face and confusion,
and how I longed to uncover and probe
the festering mystery of your lower lip.
I hear again our thoughts
whispering in the language we ought to have learned.
I hear you say, ''All of our gestures
are distracted tonight,''
over and over as the shapes of our footprints
become soft and pliant.
I cannot sleep, being deprived of that somniferous name
which once hallowed my nights.
You will not sleep
for fear of witnessing the patterns
printed on the other side of your eyelids.
This newly gained gnosis has unsettled you.
My ambition was not so chaste after all,
and your deeds were not so heroic.

Teresa Roberts

●

For the purpose of labelling,
His name will be X—
Which represents the unknown quantity.
His real name is unimportant,
But he drives a blue Oldsmobile
Which he loves above everything else,
Including his girlfriends,
Who number at least five.
On the subject of girls—
He snaps impatiently if we
Don't handle tools as quickly, as easily, as he,
And he never apologizes.
Nevertheless, if he asks us
For our brownies or sandwiches,
We say yes,
Cursing his arrogance but hoping
That after eating our food, he won't rejoin
The petite honey-haired girl
Who may become the sixth on his list...
seventh, if you count the Oldsmobile.

Teresa Roberts

FRANK AT 10 SEEN 8 YEARS LATER

His 5th grade picture hangs on my wall—
A little boy still baby-fat,
His hair redbrown like mahogany,
Not the black it is today.
His eyes are the eyes of a city kid
Transplanted young to a small town—
Not innocent, yet not worldly,
Perhaps confused.
He half smiles, half glowers.
At 10, he has not yet learned to be beautiful.

Noreen Ellis

TO SALLY THOMAS

I always watched you with mild
(actually it was a bit more)
fascination
the tough little chick with
the face of a woman
and the mouth that sang
of a bar full of drunks
or a child discovering
the forbidden fruit and loving
every bite

I saddled you with every
type of clap I could
imagine and had you
screwing with every scum
lower than yourself
you weren't pretty
but nobody overlooked you
a face hardened by the street
surrounding champagne eyes

I could never understand
why you hated me so much
or why I you

with your high
converse sneakers
and pants with one leg rolled
to the knee
beating the shit out
of girls twice your size
while you secretly counseled at Sunnyside
and me wearing
knitted scarves in August
and singing odd songs
as I entered Girl Scouts
from the side door

what children we were
that fond summer of
Busch drinking and gangfights
or running from searchlights to
the safety of the steps

and now for all my
maturity and rational sophistication
I still hate you
and wish I could be as
free, crass and loud
and able to kick your
ass from Roddy's
to the river and back again

Peter Wechsler

CITRUS FRUIT

After you slam the door against
its bruised hinges,
after the winds press and
sweep away the quinine taste
past elms & oaks through
flagrant leaves that falter,

pick up the moment
like a ripened grapefruit
in your fingers.
Press your swirling thumb,
a small Florida, in tight
against the roughened
yellow texture.

Peter Wechsler

THE GARBAGEMEN

Early Friday morning,
every Friday morning,
the distant rumble
draws closer
across the suburb.

It's no different this week;
the noise deepens in stages,
becomes a dull clamor.

I'm mostly asleep
in sheets and a blanket,
but even so, I feel
a rolling, brown sound fill my gut
and press against my sides
until the noise
is the loudest it ever gets.

They're ready
to take what they want.

Last night I lugged the barrels
out to the sidewalk—
orange peels and apple cores,
empty boxes, bottles, tinfoil,
corncobs, cartons,
steak bones picked clean.

They empty the silvery barrels
into their truck
with brilliant white gloves.

Chris Betts

RATS AT A DUEL

Black and white.
In the corner.
Rats
Are coming.
Pink eyes,
Imagine
Seeing the sun.
Damp hallways
Cause a stir.
Veins in the ears,
Red and broken,
Glow in the light
Of the sun.
Sounds of a shotgun
Ring in the background
As the duel begins.

Chris Betts

SUNSET

One
word erases
all other
words
and
skies become
clear
at night.
Psychopath
down the hall
roasting
his mother.
The sound
of daisies

in the wind
and the little
seeds
screaming.
Images
in a spoon,
my eyes
blink
at
the steamy
sunset.

Eva Iacono

7:40-2:19 WEEKDAYS

A teacher who is tall wears sweaters smokes
cigarettes, smiles baring brown teeth reddish hair
makes bundles of jokes about his wife their marriage
and sits alone in his room which has not one poster
or photograph or newspaper article is bent
over a story he had written years ago rewriting in the
margins in different color ink from the last time he had done
the same thing and wishes he was
as
as the,
as the cigarette ash falls on the corner of
a student's precis and starts a small flame.

Kai Peronard

UNCLE LOUIE

I remember when they
came and told me that Uncle
Louie would be
"going away on a trip for awhile."

This made me curious and a
little sad and I
didn't even get a chance to
say goodbye.
I wondered then who the
men in white suits
were who came and
forced Uncle into a
van one Sunday morning
while he was sitting at the
kitchen table drinking
breakfast.
And they
broke his bottle when they
dragged him and I
asked father why they were
doing that to him, and he
told me because it was
high time that it *was* done, and I
asked why was Uncle
shouting and kicking and
trying to hold on to the
things that they dragged him
by, and then clawing the
grass with his fingers, and
he, father, told me because
sometimes people don't
know what's best for them.
He came back a few months
later, much skinnier,
dressed in an old suit.
That same
night he broke into father's
bar and took some
bottles and we found him
the next
morning in the
chicken coop lying on the
sawdust snoring,
the empty bottles by his
side, a chicken by his
feet, and we pulled him
out and the

chickens watched us with their
beady wary
eyes.
The men came again and it
happened the same once
more.
So now Uncle Louie is
gone.
But I'll always
remember him on that
Sunday morning when they
took him away and how he
kicked and cursed and tried to
grab on to everything that they
dragged him by.
I remember his
face pressed against the
inside of the small
window as the
van rolled away.
I remember his
smile.
Father didn't notice it, but
Uncle Louie smiled at me, and
then he winked his
eye.

Kai Peronard

RAINY DAY

The rain is
falling with a calm
clacking past
the window where the park trees
are naked and glistening
with the dark earth.
Inside in the lazy humidity I lounge
in briefs rolled like a loincloth
and vaguely wonder why humans like

rainy days. Must be a primitive instinct:
lions didn't hunt when it poured.
I down some water and stroke
my purring cat.
A tap-tapping fills the room.
It's best to write on such days.
Life doesn't give us too many days
to just sit back and stay dry
so you try to make the most of it.
I yawn and stare at my nails.

Kai Peronard

TEENAGERAGE

The air I breathe chokes me.
The sounds I hear rattle me.
My mother's voice makes me cringe.
Everything is cement.
The toughest guys in school are after me.
Physics and trig are destroying me.
The girl I love has stopped talking to me.
My best friend hates me.
All my poems are false.
I feel like running
through the streets with a sharp knife.
I feel like going to the park
and letting loose with a gun.
I feel like hitting the wall
and smashing it down.
I feel like setting fire to my typewriter.
I feel like sleeping.
I feel like dying.
I feel like burying myself in a hole.
I wish I were young again.
I'm already seventeen.

Section Five: Since 1982

Penelope Jane Reid

A FACE LIKE YOURS

I never notice your presence
When you're in a room;
I hardly know you've been here
Until you're gone.

I don't remember your face;
The color of your eyes escapes me.
And when I try to form a picture in my mind,
It's so much larger than life
That I don't know whether it's you
I'm thinking about
Or just some character I stole out of a dream.

All I have
Is an unfocused Polaroid photograph
Of a face like yours staring
In surprise at the camera,
And the memory of a whispered half-promise
On the stairs as you were leaving.

Penelope Jane Reid

THIEF

Your hand wore another woman's ring
and yet I let you touch me.
Your words were meant for someone else
and yet I swallowed up the air in which
they rang, and let them fill me.

I broke into the safe of your passion
and took it to nourish my fantasies.

Your body wasn't mine and yet I
used it like a child who finds a coin
and promptly spends it on a bar
of Nestle's Crunch.

I feel like someone who would steal
from the Lost & Found.
I feel like someone who takes money
out of the collection plate.
I feel like someone who never tells the waitress
that she gave me too much change.

Penelope Jane Reid

SMART LIKE ME

They put me right near
the maternity ward.
I know;
they want me to see
what I've missed in my life but
I know.

the women in there all think they're
so lucky;
they're not sixteen.

The women in there
have been praying for years
for what I
just threw away.

What would he have been?
Or she?
Crazy like him.
Smart like me.

Toni Kistner

SALESMAN AFTER THE SIT

Some nights I stay
Up and wait
Sit through

The Eleven O'Clock News
Twilight Zone
Late Movie on
Channel Two

I see him through
Screen and glass
Moon highlighting
Profile; brown curls.

Tie loosened; contracts
Under right arm
What have you got on the TV?
Takes off his shoes drops
The vinyl folder and
Index cards on the
Glass dinette table
Mumbles about changing
Clothes.

Then in red
And black teeshirt
Shorts that make knees
And calves look thinner
Bonier, less professional.

Scrapes the hassock across
Green tile
Sits to face the
Television flips around
Stops at Cavett or Buckley
Goes to the refrigerator
Tears a can of Piels
From its plastic grip.

Rinses out the crystal
Shotglass makes
A peanut butter and
White bread sandwich
Grabs the bottle of Fleischmanns
By the toaster.

Sits; thighs stick
To brown vinyl cushion
Calves stick
To brown vinyl hassock
Cat sprawls across
Hairy white
Shins.

Kris Gorka

SCENE AT SANDY HOOK

It is Saturday
    (sultry Saturday)
on the beach
I stand on the edge of a blanket
putting sand on it with my feet
    & hoping I wouldn't burn
    & telling Ellen what conditioner I use—when
a girl who lives down the hall from me
approaches
    asking
"Does anyone want to take a walk with me?"
All shake their heads—and instinctively draw away
but I
say yes and
we leave
walking in silence for a while
in the shallow waves
tan little children dart around our legs
college guys
sit alone on the sand
watching the waves, or the girls,
or the boats—
some make comments to us but
we ignore them
walking in silence—she says
"You know what Danny looks like, right?"
I say no

Danny is her boyfriend—suddenly she breaks direction
and heads for the parking lot
"Maybe if I can find his car, I'll know
what beach he's on"
She stands atop a sand dune
littered
with pieces of rough wood
& empty beer bottles
& cigarette butts—
a sad silhouette punctured into
the cardboard blue sky—she
waves her arms
"Where the hell is he?" she says
I just look at her—her eyes seem to
have sunk farther into her bony face
I want to touch her
to grab her arm
to hug her
but I don't
I just look at her
"Let's walk down the road" she says
"There's a parking lot farther down"
The blacktop is hot—
she has no shoes so
she walks   arms out
balancing herself on a white painted line
"This line is going back and forth" she says
"How long have you been looking for him?"
I ask
"All day"
We continue walking—finally
she stops and
turns to me
"It's no use" she says, lifting
her sharp shoulders
"Let's go back"
We go back to the water—she sits
in the coolness, the waves slosh against her legs
Sometimes they go over them—she digs
her long fingers into the salty mud
"He's here" she says
"I know he is

I called his house
His folks said that
he was here''
She gets up and we begin to walk
apart
separated by a distance of
electric current
        a tension
a barrier
that stops me from reaching out my hand

Lori Kramer

MIRIAM

She thought it was winter
Because it was white
Like water and sleeping pills.
She'd drag and slide out of bed
Fluttering like a silver bird
Gathering in her garments.
When walking to the window
She seemed to flatten and fade
Into the light.
Like a peculiar clean shadow
Or pale pastel flower,
A little blue around the edges
With fallen petals about
Her feet in a transparent mirage.

Lori Kramer

A BOY

   She's just too wicked in her lipstick and tight bra that
smooths her breasts in a shapeless smile. She taps the table with
laughing fingernails: dreaming away the calories of her hipless
lunch. Her body is lost in nameless colours and is as hard as a

board. She cuts her hair into sharp teeth and bites anyone who doesn't lie or steal for kicks. She told me she'd rather be a boy; but I didn't believe her because she still shaves her legs and giggles about men. She told me she'd rather be a boy with no belly or thighs. I felt sorry for her. She looked so pretty when she laughed and crossed her legs. I felt sorry for her.

Kurt Lewis

GRAPEFRUIT

My grandpa had a nice lap for sitting on. When I was little, and we'd visit him in Ottumwa, I'd run to the T.V. room and find him sitting in his big easy chair, just waiting for me. I'd see his big round belly peeking out at me beneath his white T-shirt and run and jump into his lap, melding into place with his arm around me.

Grandpa liked war shows, and so did I, but Dad and Grandma didn't. Grandpa would let me stay up late and watch a movie with him. He'd take me down the long, cold hallway to the kitchen and grab a couple of grapefruits. With deep concentration he'd slice the fruit in half, the bittersweet smell stinging my nose. Then he would take great care in scooping out only the pink fleshy part but not the dividing skin. He would then squeeze the remaining juice into a bowl for me, and crown it with a sweet sheath of sugar. After I waited for this, Grandpa would grab three turnips and a beer and we would run down the hall; he'd get comfortable in his easy chair, I'd get comfortable in him, and we'd watch the show.

Every now and then Grandpa would take me to his giant bedroom with the huge fireplace. Once inside he would show me his prized possessions: bookends, his pocket watch, a shotgun, etc. Then he'd take the shotgun lovingly into his hands, stroking the fine grain of the wood, and tell me it would be mine when he died.

Grandpa's dead now, and I realize that I loved him very much. He died when I was in second grade, about ten or eleven months after my family moved up here to Minnesota. I remember when my mom came to my room in the morning before school and told me that my grandpa had passed away. The first thing I thought about was getting the shotgun, then after she told me we were leaving for Iowa in a few minutes, I thought about missing school. In the car, on the way there, I released the only feelings I had about death by singing a little song I knew: "The worms go in, the worms go out, they eat your eyes right through your snout." I remember that my dad started to cry then, but I couldn't figure out why. That was one of the two times I have ever seen him cry in my life.

Now when I think about my grandpa, and his wake, I remember his plastic shell lying in the coffin. No more round belly to lean against, but now I have a shotgun. And you know what? I don't eat grapefruit anymore, they just don't seem to taste as good.

Hedy Roma

A PEACE FOR MY MOTHER

In her green robe
velvet-like
the fraying collar
silk-like

she sits in
that crushed velvet chair
she squints at the
television

her eyes
grow smaller
less green
behind large gold rims

wire rollers
shrink her face
into a big
shiny forehead

her feet
large, bony and bare
with yellowed toenails
hang off the hassock

my father says
I should kiss
those feet
I should

Hedy Roma

SPRING OF WINTER

when for the first time
since September afternoons
the yard talks again
through white windows

and raw blueness from skies
blows past grey holes
in the screens of our bathrooms
chilling the black toilet seats

outside
brick porches are warm
but the wind still finds
holes in thin cotton pants

everyone still wears
windbreakers and wool skirts
in the morning at church
in the front pew

where a small girl
runs her dime's thin edge
up and down the sleeve of
her mother's fur coat

Mark J. Raymond

FATE OF A CHILD LOCKED IN THE PANTRY CLOSET

a child
locked in the pantry closet, dark
coffin walls lined with quiet
cans of tomato soup, green beans,
and Kraft macaroni and cheese,
with only a crack of the kitchen
light loosening the stiff air around her.
    she cowers
among the cereal boxes, the broom
lancing up with the dustpan at her side,
her heart scratching, fighting
the dark tension, the avalanche
scream inside of her bursting,
her sweet little world to end here
among the Captain Crunch and Wheaties,
the heavens to crash down
with vegetable beef and Spaghetti-o's.
    she screams
and her brother finally unlocks the door.

Mark J. Raymond

SNAPSHOT

two
polished
shells
find themselves
on the greasy rind
of a Florida beach,
abandoned there
by a pair of
multi-colored tourists

who had recently bought them
at a quaint
remodeled
gas station
which also sells oranges.

Mara Silver

GEOLOGY MUSIC

As the beats and klinks flew around
Out and down the window screen
Two giant continents crunched in time
To form the Himalayan mountains
The organ
Electric guitar synthesizers
And the bashing of land

The people and houses clicked up the guitar fingers
And muddy floating
Spoons and oboes
Were saved out of the dirt.

Mara Silver

COMFORT

How quiet must be the road where worms leap
in and out of hoops—where the black
galaxies cover each building in each city
until you can't see the lights anymore
The gigantic extension of sky that turns
to charcoal velvety warm and wraps anyone
who enters it in the special cloth. The ones
who want to get out of the sun and
noise and specks of invisible dirt that
stick to their faces, they go there. The
creatures who live at the very deep bottom

of the ocean, where you can find what
you need without a light and sand grains
aren't confusing because you can feel them
so much. The very top of the world
the outer parts—the black puzzle pieces
in the sky fit together with the
bottom of the ocean and they make a warm
dark sleeping place.

When you get there—up in the stars and down in the sea
it is black all around except for
white dots of stars, you can dart around
like an insect from tree trunk to
tree trunk and see your family and
every rock and every stratigraphic layer
and every glacier and all the spiders
and cloves and tires everything you
ever wanted to hold you
can see, protected and put in a hollow.

Sara Weiler

●

His conceit is everywhere, it follows him
like a shadow.
Pretensions
distort his actions. His features
are bloated.
The face of a fish under water.
His round mouth opens and closes
over a single vowel:
"I I I I"
        He paints his scars in purple
and deciphers them in ink
        "Here is where I cracked my skull when I was two, and
        here is where I cut my knee when I was three.

Do you see? Do you see?
These many years past
You have merely existed
But *I*
I have really lived.''

He is hollow as a conch shell,
and as beautiful.

Matthew Borczon

FOSSILS

When I was six, life was showing me the town.
I crossed streets alone, wrestled in the schoolyard,
studied my arithmetic, and prayed for three P.M.

Slowly, the flat rock of the yard becomes a fossil.
Relief marks of boys running bases and girls on swings,
even the cracked sidewalk where Tommy broke his head.

I still come to the playground. Like an archaeologist
I search the yard for my past, in the forgotten corners
where I smoked my first cigarette and lied about girls I knew.

Tonight, the current game, Sandy and a case of Mikies,
ended in a draw. Her angry, me confused.
While children play midnight baseball by the fence

I sit on the swings remembering my only home run,
straight through the Thomases' front window.
But that's typical of my games then, and now.

In ten days I'll be eighteen. Shed the skin of my youth
and leave it with the red kickballs and roller skates.
In the fossil of the playground.

Matthew Borczon

P.O.W.

Sitting on a tree stump
in the grass above the lake
wearing a p.o.w. jacket like an oxygen tent
my cigarette, an air pump,
p.o.w.
prisoner of war
prisoner of the world
Praying for winter,
cold hands scratching my cheeks red,
fluorescent evenings, knee-deep snow,
I cast my shadow across the ice
like a skater headed for Canada,
drinking your favorite wine,
repeating your favorite phrases.

A small country house,
cobblestones and red brick.
You sit in front of a large fireplace
wrapped in the arms of some new man.
Listening to Christmas carols
and talking about old lovers,
you describe me as having cat-like insincerity
and a feline cold.
He gets the picture.

Sitting on a tree stump
sentenced and condemned,
p.o.w.
prisoner of a world
where I exist as a cat,
fleas living in my ears,
drinking from my eyes.

Matthew Borczon

SUMMER NIGHTS

While they were fixing the tower of the Cathedral downtown
and replacing burned out stoplights on twelfth street
a girl slept in an abandoned car and the army
recruited two boys from Fairview.
I kissed your forehead imagining your eyes as nipples
we slept and I dreamed of rats biting at my ankles
from underneath the leaves and newspaper at Gridly park.

I woke with my feet tangled in your hair
then you made eggs said goodbye and led me to the door
the sun rises over the factory and I walk home.

Matthew Borczon

●

We made love like a parade
   and buried our hands in sand.
       I noticed the time it takes
a ship to sail over the horizon
   the tide to rise past our ankles,
      children to run by on sore feet
         then disappear.

You tell me about the driftwood tree
    you used to play on
while your nervous mother looked for sharks
      and your father talked of years
      spent with the merchant marines,

back before
      a night on the beach
      was the same as
      a night in the city.

back before
we were drawn together by our breath
with our hearts beating like band drums
while water ran between our knees.

Mark J. Borczon

JOAN OF ARC'S LAST STAND

In the room that
overlooks the
river I sat
with Joan of Arc
as she slapped rats
with the flat of
her long broadsword.

"Pesky rats" said
Joan of Arc as
she crossed herself
and swung her sword.

The stunned rodents
lay half dead on
my bedroom floor.
I throw them out
my half-open
window and smile
because I know
that Joan of Arc
is in my room.

And I'm eighteen
approaching the
age of reason
so this is the

last time I can
really believe
that Joan of Arc
would visit me.

It's so American to be this young
in desperate pursuit of having fun.

Derek Miller

•

When I'm alone in my room in the dark
I can feel the warmth of my own body
against my shirt.
Outside, beneath my window,
I can hear a dog rattling its collar,
sniffing the snow in the nighttime shadows.

Derek Miller

SLEEPLESS RESTAURANT

In the memory of a river
mallards sleep beneath the cedar trees
near the banks,
heads tucked beneath their wings.
Sticks and logs float, rot, then sink.
Mists rise from the surface in early morning
cool, to burn off,
disappearing like flights of moths
over the water at dusk,
landing, circlets echoing out
to the willow's roots.
Days, years flowing, told in the mud,
tenderly cycling,
the river changes course constantly.

Abandoned in the roadside gravel
we children will one day forget
sticking our small knives into the bark
of oaks and pines,
not to drown,
but rather to dance beneath the waters
of these fountains!

Slice
is the word for what I did to my right index finger,
the line running three-fourths of the way around it.

Restaurants that I would not recommend to anyone,
where mirrors twist your face
and photographs capture it
holding a momentary you in a sort of vise grip
for an uncomfortably long time.

It's raining so hard that the gutters
are overflowing,
the streets,
the sidewalks,
a streak of blood from my finger.
These thunderstorms,
dirty rivers
forced to search for someplace
south of here
where there's plenty of sunbaked dirt
to dry up on.

Derek Miller

YOU CAN'T EVEN FAKE IT

In Kentucky the air is different.
There's a cocktail waitress at a bar
who has blonde hair and innocent eyes.
She leans up against a wall and rubs her stomach
thinking about where everyone came from.
Her mouth smells as fresh as bluegrass.

In Colorado, in a hotel room way up in the mountains,
two Swedes lie in bed in their underwear
drinking beer and looking at the television,
talking about their parents back home
and their girlfriends
and whether or not they should clean the room
because the sliced oranges on the table
are turning bluish-green.
Swedish is a melodic language to talk about
rotting food in.

Because I hear police in the distance
because I hear my own footsteps
and the flapping of my pantlegs
and the sliding of a paper cup
across the sidewalk when I kick it,

I figure that some men in white aprons should come out
and clean this whole city
like they do in restaurants after hours.
There's nobody here at all.

Derek Miller

NOT A TORNADO WARNING

In the event of a tornado
your actions will
determine whether or not
you live or die.
Right now we are kneeling
beneath our desks,
looking at our hands.
My hands are red and swollen,
the dust is making them itch.

What is happening outside?
Do squirrels know what to do
in a tornado?
Do they have desks to dive under?
What about sparrows and herons?

Why worry about crossing the street?
The world is a big place,
and the chances of you
and an automobile
sharing the same space
at the same point in time
are very small.
Certainly smaller than the chances
of your body colliding with
a force of nature.

You are not alone,
there are eight billion Chinese
right over on the other side
of the planet, and I'm right here.
Yes, you are fragile,
you share this attribute with billions.
Now you are in one piece,
that is all that matters.

Derek Miller

LETTER TO ME OF A YEAR AGO

I have never heard the call of a peacock.
I've never even seen a peacock.
And the last time that I saw the ocean
was when I was eight years old.
I ran around picking up every shell I could find.
Now I probably wouldn't pick up any of those
sandworn skeletons,
but at eight I was so curious to look at them
and to touch them and to smell them.
Peacocks are a lot like the ocean
except that I hear the ocean all the time.

That is, I hear the ocean when I'm alone
and not talking to myself,
as I've been doing lately when I walk:

"The ground is on a tilt, this way,
so shift your weight like this. . .
watch out for the patch of ice at the bottom of this hill."
It's not amusing, and only slightly instructive,
but it is a good substitute for dreaming when I'm awake.

Speaking of dreams,
the last one that I can remember having
is one where I sat in mud
in a prison camp
watching about ten prisoners drag
two guards to a mound of dirt,
throw them down,
and shoot them in the backs of their heads.

Incidentally, I suppose you wonder why I was
thinking about peacocks in the first place.

At lunch
I sit alone
and pretend to look down at my food,
but I'm really watching all of the people,
wondering who the hell they think they are,
eating so much and talking so loud.
And I like to think of birds.

Rebecca Wolff

SLEEPHOOD

It has something to do with grasping
and something to do with teeth
and with satiation.
And it's something like
a hugh white roll of doughy stuff
that is ever-expanding
like some kind of toothpick form
that has nothing to do with what
a toothpick is.

It's something I do when I go
to sleep,
it's something that can't be done
in lighttime,
it's something like expanding fear,
it's something that's like
a love,
of some kind.
It's like a towel clenched
but not like fabric,
it's like a sight of something
that's white
but seen not with eyes,
with hands.
It's like when I'm in
that wooded room
and suddenly out of sleep.
Sounds from downstairs life
are heard from inside my ear
not from downstairs.
They're like radio waves,
like radio waves.
They begin inside my ear
and have meaning only
inside my ear.

Rebecca Wolff

SEDUCTION THEORY

Reading a lengthy article on
the seduction theory of Freud,
I am suddenly struck with the shocking realization
that it was not my brother's best friend
who attempted to penetrate my own orifice
with a plastic bag over his twig penis
when I was five years old,
or maybe a little older,
but it was my brother, himself.

Oh no, now everything is explained:
I seem to find sex an odd experience
every time, with all that flesh.
While my friends tell me their versions—
no strain or pain,
just: suddenly slender young bodies
gliding smoothly, synchronized always,
never a hitch in rhythm or
a break in concentration.

All resemblance to animals that I see
is lacking in their encounters.
There is none of the embarrassing seriousness,
the nearness to religion.
Flesh never sticks to flesh
with sweat as glue, and unwelcome noises
when pulled apart.

It was clever of me
at such a young age, I think,
to switch the roles of my attackers—
no taboos broken here, just
a horny friend of my brother's,
and he too young to object
to holding me down.

It becomes an anecdote
if told correctly, charming, with a hint
of perversion;
I was attractive even at five,
or maybe a little older.

Rebecca Wolff

RUN CATCH KISS

I was never a simple organism,
or an innocent child.
Or at least not after fourth grade,
when I knew a boy

who didn't think I was too young.
He was my best friend Wendy's
older brother, and I slept with him
when I slept over,
in a big warm bed across the small room
from Wendy and her teddy bear,
and she talked in her sleep
all night.

We played Run Catch Kiss in the gym
after school. Forget dodgeball,
this was the girls, whole feet taller, after the boys—
chase them and catch them and they were yours,
on the floor of the gym,
or inside the pitch black steamy playhouse,
or down in the basement bathrooms·
pressed up against the cold tiled wall.

My hands were shaking and I
didn't know what to do with
them, until a friend of my brother's
showed me how,
up on the loft at home.

Rebecca Wolff

THE RICH OWN US

And we know that they own
everything worth owning.
They could buy me in a second,
I've known that since I stepped through the door
of a rich girl's house
and found out that a ballgown
isn't only what Cinderella wore.
There was one on her mother
and a tuxedo on her father
and the look on her mother's face
was terror.

I heard myself bought
with her daughter's tone. It said
"I will explain later. She
is here to entertain me
for just a few hours.
You have nothing to fear,
she will disappear."

While the rich taste of bird
is still plying my tongue
like a found dollar bill, and
with butter melting and paving
the lining of my belly,
I must force myself to find
my new anger
and push my fingers towards the pen
and push my pendulum-heart towards hate.

An overfull stomach contradicts
the urge to dissent.
I did entertain her. I was
easily bought, and have disappeared.
Eat the rich.

NOTES ON CONTRIBUTORS

Katy Akin (Ma Prem Madhuri)
Berkeley, California
Hanging Loose Press published Katy Akin's book, *Impassioned Cows By Moonlight,* in 1976. She "didn't go to high school; dancing and writing were more important—engaged with great ferocity in travel, love, theater, clothes, writing, and. . .seeking." She now has found, she says, with the Bhagwan Shree Rajneesh, that place where poetry is "the. . . ground underfoot rather than a rare wild thing visiting and flying away again, leaving only a piece of paper behind."

Joanne Avallon
Phillips Academy, Andover, Massachusetts, 1979
After high school Joanne Avallon attended Tulane University for one year, then transferred to Wellesley College where she studied poetry under Frank Bidart. Her senior thesis was a book manuscript of poetry titled *vacating,* for which she received an Academy of American Poets Prize. From Wellesley, she went to Cornell University, where she has recently completed a law degree.

Carole Bernstein
Midwood High School, Brooklyn, New York, 1977
After high school, Carole Bernstein attended the University of Pennsylvania, where she studied writing with Daniel Hoffman. She continues to write poetry and to participate in a support group, "Poetry at Hardee's," named in honor of the college fast-food joint where the group first began meeting. She has published work in, among other places, *A Voyage Out* and *The Pennsylvania Review,* and she is an editor of *Painted Bride Quarterly.* Currently, she is pursuing an M.A. in the Writing Seminars Department at John Hopkins University, while working as the production manager for an international scientific and technical publisher.

Christopher Betts
East High School, Rochester, New York, 1982
Christopher Betts has been working in a bookstore since he completed a bachelor's degree in English at Wesleyan University. He says that he has gotten away from poetry but that he spends a lot of time reading novels in the hope that one day he can "actually get one down on paper."

Mark S. Borczon
Technical Memorial High School, Erie, Pennsylvania, 1984
Mark Borczon is presently studying philosophy at Edinboro
University of Pennsylvania. He says that he is ''still hard at work,
writing every day.''

Matthew Borczon
Technical Memorial High School, Erie, Pennsylvania, 1984
Like a number of other contributors, Matthew Borczon has an
interest in both writing and visual arts. He is, as this anthology
goes to press, a student at the Edinboro University of Pennsyl-
vania, majoring in art with a minor in English. He continues to
write poetry.

Tammy Boyer
Tioga Central High School, Tioga Center, New York, 1979
Tammy Boyer completed a B.A. in Music and an M.S. in Music
Education, both at Mansfield University in Pennsylvania. After
that she moved to Corning, New York, where she worked as a
part-time elementary school band teacher, while also giving
private percussion lessons and playing the drums in various
ensembles. She has now moved to Greenfield, Massachusetts,
where she is looking for a full-time teaching job. In the meantime,
she is training as a nurse's aide. And, as a new member of the
musicians' union, she is ''hoping to get some gigs very soon.''

Susan Brockman
St. Ann's School, Brooklyn, New York, 1975
Susan Brockman spends most of her time in the Bobst Library at
NYU now, surrounded by volumes of Homer, Aeschylus, and
Euripides, in the original Greek, as she prepares for oral exams as
a Ph.D. candidate in Comparative Literature at the CUNY
Gradudate Center. She finds that being a graduate student is
''pretty much a 24-hour-a-day proposition.''

Brian Butterick
Bronx High School of Science, Bronx, New York, 1974
Brian Butterick has lived ''everywhere'' from Maine to Malibu,
from Provincetown to Paris. He is presently the owner and co-
director of the Pyramid Club on Manhattan's Lower East Side.
He is one of the founding members of the art/rock band, ''3
Teens Kill 4,'' which has a mini-LP, ''No Motive,'' from Point

Blank Records, and another album on the way. He also recently made his stage debut with John Kelly in "Paved Paradise" at La Mama Etc. Theater in New York.

Kathleen Buyck
Tioga Central High School, Tioga Center, New York 1980
Kathleen Buyck graduated Magna Cum Laude from Texas Woman's University with a major in nursing and a minor in biology. She is presently living in Largo, Florida, where, as an intensive care nurse, she works with patients recovering from open heart surgery.

Bonnie Campbell
LeRoy High School, LeRoy, New York, 1978
Bonnie Campbell studied music at the University of Chicago, where she received a B.A. degree. She now lives in Massachusetts and plans to go to business school to get a degree in non-profit management.

Richard Carlin
Princeton, New Jersey, 1974
Richard Carlin has gone on to work intensively in the area of music, especially popular and folk music. He is the author of several books on music and musicology, including *The Master Collection of Dance Music* (Mel Bay), and *How to Play Portable Electronic Keyboards* (Amsco). He has also produced records for Folkways Records.

Deborah Deichler
The Baldwin School, Bryn Mawr, Pennsylvania, 1966
Since her early excursions into poetry, Deborah Deichler has become a painter. A graduate of both the Philadelphia College of Art and the Pennsylvania Academy of the Fine Arts, she has had solo exhibitions in Pennsylvania and at the Maxwell Davidson Gallery in New York City. She and her husband also operate an art transportation and delivery business in the Philadelphia area.

Mark Duckworth
McNary High School, Keizer, Oregon, 1979
After completing high school, Mark Duckworth worked full time in photographic retail, while, on the side, also doing freelance work in photography. He has had both photojournalism and

portrait work appear in several periodicals. He is continuing to do freelance work while he is presently employed in a picture framing shop. An avid guitar player, he says he is now busy composing his second song.

Noreen Ellis

Troy, New York, 1981

Noreen Ellis says that after attending four different universities in an attempt to obtain a B.A. in literature and philosophy, she found herself in Brooklyn selling bagels in a gourmet deli and trying to "force a magazine called *Leda* to fly." She has continued to write and publish her work, and the last word was that she was working on a book titled *Between Canaan and the City*. She was also looking for a new job.

Kris Gorka

Sayreville War Memorial High School, Sayreville, New Jersey, 1982

Kris Gorka received her BA in political science in 1987 from Douglass College where, she says, "I took all the writing courses they had and got done when I was a sophomore." She is still writing poetry, though uncertain of other plans, and, when last heard from, was reading *David Copperfield*.

Elizabeth Hershon

City as School, New York, New York, 1978

Elizabeth Hershon's interest in painting tends to crowd out her writing, although she is still an inveterate journal-keeper and her journal still produces poems, a number of which have appeared in *Hanging Loose*. A graduate of The School of Visual Arts, she has taught art at The Town School in New York and is the on-again, off-again night manager of Bruno's Bakery in Greenwich Village.

Jed Hershon

Various schools, Brooklyn, New York, 1982

Jed Hershon has worked in bookstores and in video production, and is presently a manager of a commercial darkroom service in New York. He was the youngest of the contributors in this book, a probable result of his enforced boyhood attendance at Hanging Loose Press editorial meetings. He sang with Dick Lourie on two albums of children's songs recorded for Folkways.

Edith Hodgkinson
Berkeley High School, Berkeley, California, 1977
Hanging Loose Press published Edith Hodgkinson's first book,
Season's Edge, in 1980. She continues to write poems and has
begun to write stories as well. "But the older I get," she says,
"the better I am at procrastinating about it." She also says that
her "mom's not too thrilled about the mad at your mother poem,
but that's what writing's all about is taking risks, right?"

William Hogeland
Saint Ann's School, Brooklyn, New York, 1973
William Hogeland was published in *Hanging Loose* when he was a
sophomore at Saint Ann's School. He later taught English there
for years before recently resigning to concentrate on writing. In
between, he attended Oberlin College, from which he graduated
in 1977. He has performed his "Poems for Two Voices" and a
series of mimes and monologues at The Kitchen, at the St.
Mark's Poetry Project, and at Franklin Furnace. His first play,
Manners, was showcased at the Harold Clurman Theater and was
given a staged reading at the 1983 Williamstown Theater
Festival.

Eve Iacono
Shoreham-Wading River High School, Shoreham, New York,
1981
Eve Iacono attended Boston University for one year, then
transfered to Amherst College, where she received a B.A. in life
sciences and anthropology. She spent four months living in a
town in the Peruvian Andes, working on an anthropological
study. Afterward, she returned to the much lower altitude of
Manhattan, where she now works in human services. She plans
to continue her social research studies in the master's degree
program at Hunter College. She says that she has taken up
running and that she recently completed her first 10 kilometer
race in Central Park.

Sam Kashner
John F. Kennedy High School, Bellmore, New York, 1972
Sam Kashner's first book of poems, *Driving at Night,* was pub-
lished by Hanging Loose Press in 1976. Since then, he has been,
among other transmigrations, a TV writer in Toronto, a student
at the Naropa Institute (a Buddhist college), and an instructor at

The Writer's Voice in New York City. He recently completed an MFA degree at Columbia University, and he has had a second collection of his work, *No More Mr. Nice Guy*, with drawings by English cartoonist Glen Baxter, published by Telephone Books. He recalls that "[*Hanging Loose* editor] Dick Lourie told me 'if you're still doing this at 35, it's serious.' I'm thirty now, and I can't imagine the next five years without a poem going on in my head."

Laura Kelsey
Penfield High School, Penfield, New York, 1977
Laura Kelsey received a B.A. in German and history from Swarthmore College. Along with her husband Gus McLeavy, she owns and operates AardBooks, a small used bookstore in Seattle, Washington. In her "abundant free time," she says that she also teaches English as a Second Language and writes poetry and prose, and, when necessary, advertising copy and feature articles. Her poems have appeared in *Hiram Review* and other small press publications. Her prose has been published in *The Antioch Review, Backbone 4,* a humor anthology, and in *Seattle VOICE.*

Toni Kistner (Throckmorton)
South Brunswick High School, Monmouth Junction, New Jersey, 1982
Toni Kistner attended NYU for two and a half years until she became disillusioned with the pursuit of a degree in English. She dropped out, began writing a novel and got married, more or less, at the same time. Now she is living in the Bath Beach area of Brooklyn with her husband and her infant son, Benjamin. Her completed novel is with a literary agent who is trying to sell it; meanwhile she is writing poems and contemplating a second novel.

Lori Kramer
Marblehead High School, Marblehead, Massachusetts, 1983
Lori Kramer is presently attending Salem State College in Massachusetts, but has plans to continue her study of British literature abroad in England. She still writes, mostly short stories these days, and has recently taken an interest in painting and baroque music.

Kate Lakoski
Wappingers Falls High School, Wappingers Falls, New York, 1976
Kate Lakoski now writes mostly for scientific journals. She is at work on her Ph.D. at Duke University, investigating how sperm acquire and develop the capacity to fertilize an egg, which she says is "fun, exciting, and even occasionally satisfying." She is also involved with local groups trying to change our country's Central America policies, something she describes as "very fulfilling, but rarely satisfying."

Kurt Lewis
Mariner High School, White Bear Lake, Minnesota, 1982
Kurt Lewis went straight to college after high school, but didn't like it, and only stayed a year. As this anthology went to press, he was working in Germany, and planning to stay there a while longer.

Susan Mernit
Great Neck South Senior High School, Great Neck, New York, 1969
After teaching creative writing at Hunter College for three years, Susan Mernit left that job in 1986 to work full-time as a freelance writer. She now writes regularly for *The New York Times Book Review, Working Woman, Woman's World, McCall's, MD, Small Press, Poets & Writers Magazine,* and other publications. Her books include *The Angelic Alphabet* and *Tree Climbing.* She lives in Brooklyn with her husband and their son, Zachary Nathan Jarrett.

Derek Miller
Cranbrook High School, Bloomfield Hills, Michigan, 1985
Derek Miller studied poetry with Faye Kicknosway and Ken Mikolowski while he was still in high school. He went on to study at the University of Michigan. But three months of that experience, he says, made him skeptical about the value of formal education and he dropped out. At this point, he has moved to downtown Detroit, where he is working at the Detroit Public Library, writing poems, and "enjoying being alive." He recently gave a public reading from his work at the Library.

Naomi Miller
Saint Ann's School, Brooklyn, New York, 1971
Naomi Miller works as a psychotherapist in a holistic health center in New Jersey. She is also pursuing a Ph.D. at Rutgers-Newark, doing research on the phenomenal experience of time. She is active in anti-nuclear politics and lives with a small group of people on a "pretty piece of land." She says that she spends "a great deal of time splitting wood and tinkering with the tractor."

Gerry Pearlberg
Stuyvesant High School, New York, New York, 1979
Gerry Pearlberg still writes poems and "even publishes them, from time to time." She is on the editorial collective of *Heresies: A Feminist Publication of Art & Politics,* and is active in a variety of political pursuits. She lives in Brooklyn with her cat, Max, and is the Project Director of the Women and AIDS Project at the Women's Action Alliance, Inc.

Kai Peronard
Brooklyn, New York, 1982
Kai Peronard says that what he has been "doing" since high school is "reassessing my human existence, trying to pay my bills, stay in school, develop a prose style, develop a poetic style . . . ." While a film student at New York University, he has been writing screen plays and shooting footage; at the same time, he has been working on the campus newspaper, *The Washington Square News.* The last word from him was that he was planning a trip to Chile, where he was born, and reading a lot of Neruda in preparation.

Joan Polikoff
Highland Park, Illinois, 1979
After completing her degree in literature from Yale University, Joan Polikoff embarked on a trip throughout Europe. She last wrote to us as she was leaving from Paris for County Galway, Ireland.

Allison Polly
The Masters School, Dobbs Ferry, New York, 1982
Allison Polly recently graduated from Brown University where she majored in psychology and minored in film. While at Brown, she also studied fiction and playwriting and wrote short stories

and a one act play. She is currently working at a media center in New York, where she is conducting a research project on films for children. The results will be published in *Young Viewers Magazine*.

Mark J. Raymond
Rockland District High School, Rockland, Maine, 1983
Mark J. Raymond is completing his undergraduate studies at Bates College in Lewiston, Maine. Writing remains a central focus in his life, but, with the exception of contributions to his college literary magazine, he hasn't attempted to publish either his poems or his prose work.

Penelope Jane Reid
J.M. Atherton High School, Louisville, Kentucky, 1983
Penelope Reid recently graduated from Indiana University at Bloomington with a degree in journalism and classical studies. The last we heard from her, she was copy desk chief for the *Indiana Daily Student*.

Michael Rezendes
Westledge High School, Simsbury, Connecticut, 1971
Michael Rezendes earns his living these days as a freelance writer. He was the editor of the *East Boston Community News* from 1979 to 1981, a staff writer for the *Boston Phoenix* from 1981 to 1984, and, more recently, has been a political writer for the San Jose *Mercury News*. He has published articles in a wide variety of places, including the *Boston Globe, Columbia Journalism Review*, *The Nation*, and *The Washington Post*. He confesses that he "hasn't written a poem since 1976," but adds that he is "putting a novel together, working under the premise that in the end, the fiction will carry more weight than the journalism."

Tim Robbins
Greensburg Community High School, Greensburg, Indiana, 1982
One of *Hanging Loose's* most frequent contributors as a high school student, Tim Robbins has continued to write, publish and study—at the University of Indiana and on his own. He spent his junior year abroad in France and other places. Now, as a recent graduate, he has turned his attention to German, after previously studying French, Hebrew and Chinese. He says that when he is not studying or enjoying the company of his friends, he reads

poetry and listens to music: Edith Piaf, Sarah Vaughan, Billie Holiday, and Bob Dylan are among his favorites.

Teresa Noelle Roberts
Cortland High School, Cortland, New York, 1981
After graduating from Hamilton College, Teresa Roberts moved to Brooklyn where she lived flanked by the East River on one side and the Greenwood Cemetery on the other, while working as a publicist in a children's book company. Recently she moved back to the Finger Lakes region of New York State, where she grew up, in order to "work on a novel, reacquaint myself with trees, clean air and snow that isn't grey, and learn to sail on Cayuga Lake." And to get a job. Her poems have appeared in *Deviance, Proofrock, Room of Our Own, Sojourner*, and other publications.

Hedy Roma
Sayreville War Memorial High School, Sayreville, New Jersey, 1982
After undergraduate studies at New York University in art history and economics, Hedy Roma made the practical choice, and is presently a graduate student at NYU in art history; her special interest is in the baroque. She has continued writing in her notebooks, though not for publication, and one of her long-range goals is to put this writing together in some cohesive form.

Heather Ryan
Cambridge Latin High School, Cambridge, Massachusetts, 1979
Heather Ryan has made the transition from Cambridge to San Francisco, where, the last we heard, she was working for an "entrepreneur who comes up with new (and taxing, for his assistants) ideas almost daily." She continues to write, mostly fiction now.

Mike Shulman
Scarsdale High School, Scarsdale, New York, 1976
Mike Shulman continued to write poems in college and published some of them in the student literary magazine, while an undergraduate at Wesleyan University. But when, in his junior year, he could find little support on campus for his writing, he turned his attention instead to psychology. He has since completed his Ph.D. in clinical psychology at the University of Michigan. He is currently doing post-doctoral work at the Detroit Psychiatric

Institute, and recently published a paper on the psychoanalytic theory of the id. He says that he continues to read poetry and hopes to get back to writing poetry again, soon.

Mara Silver
Mohawk Trail Regional High School, Buckland, Massachusetts, 1983
Mara Silver recently graduated from the College of the Atlantic in Bar Harbor, Maine, with a degree in Human Ecology. In the summers, she has had a job in "the wild gardens of Acadia" in Acadia National Park. She continues to write poems, but says she hasn't tried to publish any work lately, and also works in ceramics.

Rob Solomon
Saint Ann's School, Brooklyn, New York, 1971
Robert Solomon lives in Brooklyn, New York, where he is in the cabinet-making business. He says that he hasn't written much poetry or prose lately, and hasn't published any work since he finished high school.

Lawrence Stazer
Saint Ann's School, Brooklyn, New York, 1977
Lawrence Stazer is a fictitious name. The poems were written by a group of Robert Hershon's students at Saint Ann's School in Brooklyn: *Kate Brodtkorb, Dan Brody, Justine Cassell, Tom Fogler, Peter Hamburger, Colette Johnson, Katie Merz, Michael Mok, Danny Rosenblatt, Peter Rothe, Elise Smith,* and *Blake Taylor.* The collaboration included group poems, parodies, borrowings, and a variety of other techniques.

Sarah Waddell
The Masters School, Dobbs Ferry, New York, 1982
As this anthology went to press, we had no further information about this writer.

Peter Wechsler
Milton Academy, Milton, Massachusetts, 1979
Peter Wechsler worked on the literary magazine at Milton Academy and was president of the debating team. After completing high school, he attended Princeton University.

Sara Weiler
Concord Academy, Concord, Massachusetts, 1984
Sara Weiler completed four years of high school but never actually graduated. Nevertheless, she went on to study painting and drawing at the Museum School (at the Museum of Fine Arts) in Boston. After one year, she moved to the west coast to continue her studies at the San Francisco Art Institute. She is presently living again in her home town of Cambridge, Massachusetts and working as a caterer and as a waitress, in order to amass large sums of money as quickly as possible so that she can "have adventures"—in Europe and elsewhere. She continues to write from time to time in a form she describes as "not as loose as poetry, but not as tight as prose."

Rebecca Wolff
Stuyvesant High School, New York, New York, 1983
Rebecca Wolff grew up in New York City, until the age of 16 when she moved herself to Cape Cod. After high school, she made her way through one and a half years at Bennington College in Vermont. Now she is living in Boston, which she finds "a much easier place to be." There she is working at a natural foods supermarket and continuing to write poems. She published her first poem in *Seventeen* at the age of fifteen, several poems in *Hanging Loose* at the age of seventeen, and now, at the age of nineteen, will have a poem soon in the British journal *Psychopoetica*.

Joseph Szabo (cover photographs) is on leave from the faculty of the International Center of Photography. His work is in the collections of ICOP, the Museum of Modern Art, the Metropolitan Museum of Art, the Brooklyn Museum, and others. Szabo's photographs have appeared in such journals as *U.S. Camera, The Library of Photography*, and *Popular Photography*. His book, *Almost Grown*, features photographs of Long Island teenagers, with a text edited by Alan Ziegler, and he has recently compiled a new collection, of adolescent girls, from which our cover pictures are drawn. Szabo's awards include a Fellowship from the National Endowment for the Arts.

Dick Lourie's poems have been published in many magazines and anthologies and in several collections of his own work. He is a founding member of the New York State Poets in the Schools; for the last 20 years he has been a teacher and curriculum consultant for poets-in-the-schools programs in New York, New Jersey, and Massachusetts. He received his B.A. in English from Princeton University, his M.A. in American literature from Columbia University, and his ME.d. in reading from Harvard University.

Mark Pawlak's poetry and his translations from the German of Bertolt Brecht and others have appeared widely, and two collections of his own work have been published. He has taught science, mathematics, and poetry, in public and private elementary and secondary schools, and has worked as poet in residence for the public schools of Worcester, Massachusetts. He received his B.S. in physics from MIT, and he currently teaches mathematics at the University of Massachusetts at Boston.

Robert Hershon has taught writing for Teachers & Writers Collaborative and for Saint Ann's School in New York, among others. Nine collections of his own poems have been published and his awards include a National Endowment for the Arts Fellowship. He is executive director of the Print Center, Inc., a non-profit organization for educational and arts printing.

Ron Schreiber edited the anthology *31 New American Poets* and five books of his own poems have been published. He is a Professor of English at the University of Massachusetts-Boston, where he has taught since 1968, serving as Chair of the Department in 1985-1988.

The editors of Hanging Loose wish to thank their two former colleagues, Emmett Jarrett and Miguel Ortiz, both of whom served as editors during the time when many of the poems in this anthology were first selected to appear in the magazine, and whose efforts, consequently, have helped give shape to the present collection.